change anything

THE NEW SCIENCE
of PERSONAL SUCCESS

Kerry Patterson, Joseph Grenny, David Maxfield,
Ron McMillan and Al Switzler

piatkus

PIATKUS

First published in the US in 2011 by Business Plus, an imprint of
Grand Central Publishing
First published in Great Britain in 2011 by Piatkus

Copyright © 2011 by VitalSmarts, LLC

The moral right of the author has been asserted.

A CIP catalogue record for this book
is available from the British Library.

ISBN 978-0-7499-5568-7

Printed and bound in Great Britain by
Clays Ltd, St Ives plc

Piatkus
An imprint of
Little, Brown Book Group
100 Victoria Embankment
London EC4Y 0DY

An Hachette UK Company
www.hachette.co.uk

www.piatkus.co.uk

We dedicate this book to

Albert Bandura

Contents

Part I: The Science of Personal Success

When people can't change, it's rarely because they lack the
will. It's usually because they're blind and outnumbered:
They're blind to all but one or two of the six sources of
influence that make them do what they do. And there are
far more invisible sources of influence working against
them than there are visible sources acting in their favor.
Our research shows that people who learn to see and use all
six sources of influence are ten times more likely to create
profound, rapid, and lasting change in their lives and the
lives of others.

Change happens when we stop looking for off-the-shelf answers
to our one-of-a-kind challenges. You are unique.

The change plan that will work for you is unique. In order to find it, you'll have to be both the scientist and the subject of your unique experiment. When you take on this mind-set, even bad days become good data. You become progressively smarter at influencing yourself until you evolve a plan that works perfectly for your subject: *you*.

Part II: The Six Sources of Influence

If you are ever to succeed at changing—and staying changed—you'll have to learn to disarm your impulses and make the right choices pleasurable. The only way you can sustain change is to change what brings you pleasure. How do we learn to change our likes?

If change is taking too much will, it's probably because you lack skill. When change seems hard, we blame our character, but our character is usually not to blame. We are blind to the crucial role *skills* play in creating and sustaining change. The problem is not that you're weak—it may be that you're ignorant. There's a difference! Ignorance can be fixed—and surprisingly quickly. With just a few weeks of *deliberate practice*, you can master skills that make change easy and permanent.

Bad (and good) habits are a team sport—they require lots of *accomplices* to start and sustain. Few people have any idea how many others are involved in undermining their efforts to change through encouraging and enabling bad choices. If you want to change your behavior, you'll have to turn a few accomplices into friends. More often than not, the transformation can happen with a single *crucial conversation*. Eliminate a few accomplices and add as few as two new friends to your influence strategy, and your odds of success increase as much as 40 percent.

Bad habits are often surprisingly cheap—in the short term. Also, human beings value pleasure today much more than they fear punishment tomorrow. You can use your own irrationality in a positive way by inverting this economy. Surprisingly, you can reverse incentives by bribing yourself to change—and it works! You can also reverse costs by raising the price of bad behavior. Research shows that you can dramatically change your own behavior by putting a bit of skin in the game.

We're blind to the hundreds of ways our environment controls us. Our surroundings powerfully control what we think, how we feel, and how we act. If you want to take control of your life, you have to take control of your surroundings. Learn to use distance, cues, and tools in your favor, and you enlist the environment as a powerful, constant, and sleepless ally.

Part III: How to Change Anything

Skillful Changers have created vital behaviors and engaged all six sources of influence to dramatically improve results with colleagues and loved ones and in themselves. Learn how real people have integrated all of the strategies and tactics of the new science of personal success into an effective change plan in achieving career success, weight loss, financial fitness, addiction recovery, or relationship renewal.

Preface

Our Promise

The promise of this book is simple. If you apply the principles and tactics we outline, you can rapidly, profoundly, and sustainably change your own behavior (even long-standing bad habits). And by learning how to change your own behavior, you can dramatically improve results in most any area of life.

To discover what it takes to change how one behaves, we at the Change Anything Labs examined the struggles and strategies, trials, and triumphs of more than five thousand people—all of whom were searching for ways to overcome personal challenges. These intrepid searchers were looking to

- **Accelerate their careers.** Eighty-seven percent of the employees we surveyed reported that they have been passed over for promotions or pay increases because they were unable to make the changes their bosses had requested. All understood that they needed to change their behavior, but they weren't sure how to do it.[1]

- **Become financially fit.** Fewer than one in five adults believe that they are tending to their personal finances in a way that will secure their futures—and their primary barrier to success is their own behavior. All knew they needed to spend less and save more, but none were certain how to get themselves to do that.[2]

- **Save a struggling relationship.** Our research into 350 relationships on the brink of failure revealed that relationships don't fail because of *chemistry*; they fail because of *behavior*. Those who regain and deepen their friendship or intimacy succeed by changing how they treat their friends and loved ones.[3]

- **Thrive in the midst of organizational change.** Many subjects were struggling to adapt to challenging changes imposed on them by their employers. Many felt like victims of these involuntary demands—but some examined the changes strategically and adapted to them in ways that restored their sense of control and even improved their professional prospects.

- **Lose weight, get fit, and stick with it.** The number one cause of illness and death today is neither viral nor genetic. It's behavioral. Individuals who succeed at getting off the diet treadmill don't discover a magic pill or an all-powerful tool; instead, they create a robust plan for change that creates lifelong habits of health and wellness.

- **Break free of addictions.** Overcoming addiction isn't just about finding a cure; it's about changing seemingly intractable habits.[4] Those who succeed at kicking debilitating addictions do so because, whether they know it or not, they apply the science of personal success to their own challenges.

As we examined these everyday people in the throes of either overcoming addictions or improving failing careers and relationships, we found hope. Hundreds of people in our study (we'll call them Changers) not only succeeded in changing their unhelpful habits, but also maintained these changes for at least three years. We were particularly interested in this vital group, so we studied them carefully—and from them we learned the science behind personal success. That's because whether you find them in Kilungu, Kenya, or Carmel, California—or whether they're dealing with an alcohol addiction or an indolent lifestyle—all of the Changers drew on the same principles of influence.

Now, as successful as they were, many of them lamented how long it took them to succeed in their change. Our Changers tenaciously stumbled their way into success in the way anyone who succeeds will have to. What you'll learn in this book, however, is that with a little more study, you can do a lot less stumbling. When you understand the science behind their success, you can be much more deliberate in your attempts and efficient in your progress. The principles and tactics we outline in this book will enable you to intentionally apply what others only struggled to discover—dramatically accelerating your progress on your path to success.

And success *will* be yours. Our most recent research revealed that those who apply what you are about to learn are not just marginally more effective at bringing about change; they are exponentially so. In fact, those who apply the science of personal success are more than 1,000 percent more successful at producing change than those who try other means.[5]

And now for the final piece of good news. Whether you're trying to change a habit in your work or personal life, you'll receive benefits on both fronts. For example, many of the individuals we studied experienced a challenge in their personal life that, by their own calculations, also dragged down their work performance by as much as 50 percent.[6] In their case, fixing one problem meant fixing two. Our Changers likewise reported that improving their lot at work created benefits that relieved stress and increased confidence at home as well. Changers are almost always twice blessed.

So take hope as you get ready to learn more about the science of personal success. People can and do change—and stay on course for years thereafter. By following in their footsteps, you too can become a Changer. And once you do—once you learn the principles and skills of personal change—you can change anything.

Your Complimentary Subscription to ChangeAnything.com

With the purchase of this book, you now have exclusive access to ChangeAnything.com, a dynamic website that helps people make changes in their personal and professional lives. You'll notice references to this site throughout the book. From weight loss to corporate change initiatives, ChangeAnything.com combines the best social science research with the principles of social media to ensure your change effort is successful. You will find an ID code inside your book cover. Log on to www.ChangeAnything.com/exclusive and use your code to sign up for a free limited-time premium subscription. It's that easy to get started.

Acknowledgments

Each book we write reminds us of the large debt of gratitude we owe to so many.

Our first heartfelt thanks goes to

- Our families, whose support and love has been unwavering
- Our colleagues at VitalSmarts and ChangeAnything.com for committed, brilliant contributions in helping us achieve our mission
- Our associates, master trainers, and international partners, who so professionally represent VitalSmarts to clients around the world
- The dedicated trainers who deliver Crucial Conversations, Crucial Confrontations, and Influencer training with both skill and heart
- The selfless individuals who have helped with our research— through surveys, interviews, and experiments at the Change Anything Labs

- The brilliant scholars whose work points the way to better lives for all of us.

We'd also like to personally thank

- Mindy Waite, our chief editor and secret literary weapon at Vital-Smarts
- Margaret Maxfield and T.P. Lim, early readers who shared insightful feedback
- Rick Wolff, our executive editor, and now colleague, at Business Plus
- Kevin Small—"agent" is too small a word; a man with a great soul and keen mind for making a difference in the world
- Andy Shimberg, Mary McChesney, Brittney Maxfield, Mike Carter, James Allred, and Rich Rusick—colleagues at VitalSmarts who, after the writing is done, lead the charge in taking the book to the world.

If this book does some good in the world, we hope these individuals feel a measure of satisfaction from knowing that they were instrumental in all of it.

change anything

PART I
THE SCIENCE OF PERSONAL SUCCESS

Escape the
Willpower Trap

Any book that claims that it can help you change *anything* in your personal and professional life—from increasing your disposable income, career options, and physical fitness, to decreasing your smoking, food intake, and relationship struggles—had better be based on careful scientific inquiry. It had better report results—to three decimal places. Most of all, any recommendations it makes had better come from careful study of human subjects—not just rodents or simians.

With this in mind, we'll start our journey down the trail of personal success with a rather engaging piece of scientific inquiry into the habits of real people. This particular experiment was conducted at the Change Anything Labs nestled at the base of the Wasatch Mountains of Utah. It is in this lab that we conduct research, pore over contemporary social science findings, and interview people we call Changers. Changers are individuals who once faced enormous personal challenges, wrestled them to the ground, and have remained successful for at least three years. These Changers and this research provide us with both the practical advice and the scientific results people need to not only change, but change for good.

This particular day, we used the Change Anything Labs to conduct a rather fascinating study. There, in a room by himself, sat a four-year-old boy named Kyler. We were examining his ability to resist temptation, and from the strained look on his face, it looked as if he just might lose. To test his ability to delay gratification, we seated Kyler across the table from a formidable foe—a scrumptious marshmallow.

Five decades ago, the legendary psychologist Walter Mischel demonstrated that kids who could sit down with a marshmallow in front of them and *not eat it* for a full fifteen minutes did better in almost every area of life than more impulsive kids who scooped up the treat and ate it right away—in spite of the fact that they were all instructed to wait.

As Mischel followed his research subjects for the next two decades, he learned that children who delayed gratification eventually scored hundreds of points higher on standardized school tests. They also had stronger relationships, were promoted more often, and were happier. Mischel showed that the capacity to delay gratification is, indeed, a big deal.

THE WILLPOWER TRAP

Unfortunately, to this day most people draw the wrong conclusion from this study. They fall into what might best be called "the willpower trap."

They assume that the *only reason* (among many possible reasons) certain kids were better at delaying gratification than others was that nature had endowed them with more willpower. Period. The research subjects who withstood temptation showed more moxie or strength of character. It's little wonder that their lives unfolded in happier and more successful ways. They were innately stronger.

This is the same simplistic assumption most of us make when explaining why we fail to change our own bad habits. When we fall off the wagon, go on a shopping spree, give in to our hair-trigger temper with a co-worker, procrastinate over work tasks, or binge eat, we blame our failure on a lack of willpower. We obviously just don't *want it* badly enough. We don't push ourselves to the limit. Of course, when we succeed, we brag about our grit, tenacity, and commitment. Either way, when explaining why we do what we do, we see, think about, and eventually blame or give credit to one thing—our willpower.

This simplistic view is not only wrong; it's tragically wrong. It's wrong because it's incomplete. And it's tragic because it gives us nowhere to go when we struggle to change our own bad habits or improve our lot. When people believe that their ability to make good choices stems from nothing more than their willpower—and that willpower is a quality they're either born with or they're not—they eventually stop trying altogether. The willpower trap keeps them in a depressing cycle that begins with heroic commitment to change, which is followed by eroding motivation and terminated inevitably by relapse into old habits. Then, when the built-up pain of their bad habits becomes intolerable, they muster up another heroic but doomed attempt at change. We feel as if we were ascending a summit when in fact we're simply walking a treadmill: lots of effort, no progress. That's the willpower trap.

Fortunately, Mischel's research goes further than most of us realize. A few years after his original study, he and Albert Bandura (another titan of psychology) asked a crucial question. They wondered if what appeared to be *will* might, in fact, be more a function of *skill*. The two scholars suspected that the kids who controlled their cravings weren't simply more *motivated* than those who gave in to their temptation, but were more *able*. They had learned a skill or two along the way.[1]

This was an important issue to settle, because if Mischel and Bandura had it right, it would mean that failure to harness one's impulses is *not* fixed at birth. Although grit and its close cousin character may be genetic, *skills* can actually be learned. This alternate explanation offers hope to all of us. It's also the reason we were studying Kyler and twenty-seven of his four-year-old peers in the Change Anything Labs. We wanted to know if we could teach contemporary children skills that help them actively delay gratification rather than sit back and hope they won the willpower lottery.

To test our theory, we replicated Mischel's original experiment. We asked a group of kids to sit in front of a marshmallow and promised them that if they resisted eating the treat for fifteen minutes, we'd give them a second sugary treat. These kids made up the control group, and to nobody's surprise, they performed just as the original subjects had in 1962. About a third of the subjects gutted it out for fifteen minutes. The other two-thirds lunged for the sweet.

The plot thickened as we brought in the experimental group—Kyler and thirteen other four-year-olds. We made Kyler's group the same offer, but this time we taught them skills they could use if they wanted to wait. Rather than simply instructing them to hunker down, we taught them to use distance and distractions to influence their own behavior. (To watch these rather charming subjects as they face down their marshmallows, visit ChangeAnything.com/exclusive.)

Here's where it got interesting. Six minutes into the experiment, Kyler knitted his brow as he appeared to imagine the first delicious contact between the marshmallow and his tongue. He started to melt into submission. But then the skills we taught Kyler kicked in. He turned his body away from his nemesis and began mouthing the words to a story his parents often tell him before bedtime. He was doing anything he could to distance and distract himself—helping supplant his need for will.

A few minutes later, Kyler exited the Change Anything Labs proudly clutching a marshmallow in each hand. He had succeeded. "I did it!" he proclaimed as he stuffed the two marshmallows into his mouth. In fact, 50 percent more kids were successful at holding out for the second marshmallow when taught a couple of distraction skills—demonstrating that one of the biggest barriers to personal success is not one's lack of moxie, chutzpah, or willpower, but the mistaken belief that willpower is *the* key to change.

WE'RE BLIND

What do we learn from Kyler and his friends? Mastering temptations is not solely a function of *personal motivation*. When it comes to changing our behavior, skills also play an important role. That means that the model of human behavior that most of us carry around in our heads—the model we use to figure out how to change our own habits—is woefully incomplete. By relying on our handy but incomplete tough-it-out model, we routinely ignore the many sources of influence that are working for and against us—*personal ability* to name just one. As it turns out, there are lots of different forces out there that are acting on us all the time.

You yourself may have fallen into the willpower trap. For instance, if you're currently trying to give up smoking, alcohol, or drugs, wouldn't simply going cold turkey be your shortest route to success? The same is true when it comes to withstanding the temptation to buy the latest electronic device, or keeping your temper with a loved one, or getting up early to study for a course you're taking to better your career. Just gut it out and you'll do fine, right?

The problem here isn't that you believe in the importance of willpower for creating personal change. Willpower obviously plays a role in our choices. The problem arises when you rely exclusively on a tough-it-out model and ignore the legion of other sources of influence that are working for and against you.

For example, when you walk into a casino in Las Vegas or Macao, you're practically assaulted by the crass influence methods the owners employ to separate you from your next rent payment. For instance, the hotel registration counter lies at the back of the casino, so you have to walk through a labyrinth of tempting game tables and cool-looking slot machines just to get a room. Then there are the chips you see in such abundance. Social scientists have shown that you'll lose chips more willingly than you'll let go of cash, so the casino owners insist that you play with chips.[2] And who can miss the exciting sound of other people winning—Bing! Bang! Cha-ching! Oh boy, maybe you can win too!

These influence techniques are fairly easy to spot, but take care, because there are lots of other more subtle techniques in play—all carefully designed by individuals who have one goal: to separate you from your money. Casino designers manipulate the type and level of the music playing in the background, the colors and shape of the room, the length of the arms of the slot machines, the color and pattern of the carpet (they install carpets that are so visually jarring that patrons look up and away from them and toward the slots). The methods of influence are nearly endless.

When it comes to more routine human activity, such as eating, drinking, interacting with co-workers, and shopping, you could fill a library with books that explain how people are working feverishly to get you to act in ways that bring them billions of dollars in profits while giving you unwanted pounds, a failed liver, divorce, and bankruptcy.

For instance, did you know that the sound that's most likely to get your attention is the sound of a baby giggling? A baby giggles, and everyone turns to see. Sound experts know this, and they use it to their advantage in advertising.[3] Did you realize that there was a time when the organist at the North Rim Grand Canyon Lodge played peppier music when the restaurant line grew—influencing people to eat faster and get out of the restaurant sooner than they had originally planned?[4] Do you think the patrons realized that they had just wolfed down a meal that they had intended to enjoy at their leisure—because the music hustled them along? It's doubtful.

That's why when it comes to personal change, we first think of our own lack of motivation. Our primary problem isn't that we're weak; it's that we're blind—*and when it comes to long-standing habits, what you can't see is usually what's controlling you.*

Also, since we can't see how many sources of influence are working against us, we blame our setbacks on the one source of influence we can spot—ourselves. This particular source of personal influence is obvious, handy, and simple to consider. Plus, if our problems stem from our lack of personal motivation, that puts us in the driver's seat. We can whip ourselves into a motivational lather and head off in search of change—for a while.

WE'RE OUTNUMBERED

Fortunately, when it comes to combating the myriad forces that encourage us to overeat, overreact, overspend, lounge too much, smoke, drink too much, sleep too much, and play video games too much, we don't always respond with a call for more willpower. We try other influence methods as well. We tinker with an exercise bike, try a stop-smoking patch, put up a motivational poster, take training courses, and so forth. The bad news is that more often than not we bring these influence tools into play one at a time. Little good that does. The forces that are working against us are legion—and they work in combination. So when it comes to solving personal problems, people are not only blind; they're also outnumbered.

To see how your typical change effort takes form, consider the following metaphor. Your rather large SUV runs out of gas a half block from a gas station—just over a gently cresting hill. You decide to push the beast to the nearest pump, but this isn't your old, tinfoil-based VW bug that you could easily push by yourself; it's the Sherman tank of soccer moms. So you wave down a half dozen rather large and muscular strangers to help you. Each puts in a full effort. Each grunts and strains and pushes against the massive bulk—*one person at a time*. In response, your SUV just sits there with a smug look on its grille.

Now, as hopeless as this example sounds, it's about to get worse.

Imagine that in addition to the fact that the people assisting you are working in isolation rather than in combination, there are six hefty strangers all pushing together to propel your truck back *down* the hill. Now you have an accurate image of why your change attempt feels so overwhelming. Our problem is not just that we're using only one source of influence at a time; it's also that those who aren't pushing for us are usually pushing against us.

This is precisely why we fail in our attempts at personal change. There may be half a dozen sources of influence sustaining our old bad habits, and we muster just one clever strategy at a time to offset this overwhelming combination. Then we act shocked when our anemic idea falls short—and set out to punish the "slacker" who authored it: ourselves. It's a hopeless, discouraging trap.

IF YOU CAN SEE IT, YOU CAN CHANGE IT

So how can you get both vision and numbers working in your favor? Kyler and his marshmallow-resisting friends give us a hint of what can happen. After learning a couple of simple skills, 50 percent more of the experimental subjects were able to resist the temptation. When they added a little skill to their existing will, their odds of success shot up substantially. Could the same thing work for adults? When it comes to fighting our own personal demons, what if we could match the multiple sources that are working against us with multiple sources of our own?

To answer these questions, we'll return to the Change Anything Labs. In this experiment we'll collaborate with a teenage scientist named Hyrum who wondered whether older kids could be as easily blinded and outnumbered as adults. His research team blitzed ten-year-olds with six sources of influence to see if this affected their behavior. The team also examined the question of whether the kids were aware of what had happened to them.

To test the power of multiple sources of influence, the research team designed an experiment to tempt kids to do what many adults routinely do—spend themselves into bankruptcy in spite of their best intentions to save for the future. The study started on a Saturday morning as a group of nervous parents watched their preteens on a closed-circuit TV monitor. The adults knew that the researchers would be attempting to influence their children to save or spend money—depending on the luck of the draw—and were anxious to see how they would fare. Would their child be a spendthrift or a fiscally responsible money manager? Inquiring parents wanted to know.

As each child entered the lab, Hyrum explained the upcoming activity. Each kid would be given a "career" that would last ten minutes and include four simple tasks. The kids would be paid ten dollars for completing each task. If they did as they were told, they could earn up to forty dollars. Hyrum also warned them that they'd be offered opportunities along the way to spend their earnings. To help them resist these temptations, he invited them to think about what they would like to do with forty dollars once they returned home.

As the kids talked about the money they could earn, it was clear that they all had exciting plans for the loot. They all seemed motivated to resist the temptation to spend.

Then, one at a time, the kids began their careers. They were surprised at how simple it was to make money. In the first task they ranked assorted candies from least to most favorite. That was a no-brainer. For their second task they alphabetized toys. What could be easier?

After each task, Hyrum paid the subjects ten dollars and invited them to have a look at the Change Anything Store. The store consisted of a countertop covered with inexpensive candies and toys. The first thing the shoppers noticed was that prices were five to ten times what they would pay in a regular store. For example, a bag of Skittles was marked at eight dollars. Not only were the prices outrageous, but the kids *knew* they were outrageous.

So, here's the situation. The research subjects had big plans for their money. The only temptation they faced was the opportunity to buy sweets and toys at ridiculous prices. And here's what we wanted to know: Would their choices be affected by six different sources of influence? And if so, would the kids even notice it?

The answer to the first question—Could their spending actions be influenced at all?—was an unequivocal yes. The first fifteen kids in the study emerged from the lab with less than thirteen (of the possible forty) dollars in their pockets. A couple of the kids left with only the shirts on their backs and a handful of overpriced goodies.

One excited buyer spent his entire fortune on Silly String. His mother later reported that as they left, the boy stared sadly at the cans in his arms and lamented, "I'm so stupid! I could have had forty bucks! But now all I have is this dumb Silly String."

But not everyone spent lavishly. A second group of fifteen kids saved an average of thirty-four of their forty dollars. This group of subjects completed the same tasks in the same room with the same store offering sweets and toys at the same prices, but they took home two-and-a-half times what the first group did! What happened? Were they genetically blessed with more willpower? Did they see the forces working against them and take steps to counteract them?

Let's pull back the curtain and see what was really going on. We'll start by exploring the spenders' thinking. One by one we asked them about their outlandish purchases. Each was quite aware of the retail value of their overpriced goods. They knew they had pretty much thrown their money away. *But they didn't recognize the forces that had caused them to spend so freely.* Instead, they fell into the willpower trap by blaming themselves. One child appeared baffled by his own actions, reporting, "I'm not sure what happened. I guess I must have really wanted this."

And it wasn't just the spenders who didn't know what had hit them. The savers were equally unaware of the forces that had propelled them to save. While the spenders took too much of the blame, the savers took too much of the credit. They figured they had shown more discipline because they were strong, motivated, and goal oriented.

Both groups were wrong.

SIX SOURCES OF INFLUENCE

So what actually caused the profound differences in spending? The research team at the Change Anything Labs manipulated six different sources of influence to affect the subjects' behavior—the same sources of influence that operate on *you* twenty-four hours a day. With the first group (the spenders), six sources were used to promote spending. With the second group (the savers), the same sources were used to promote saving.

Here's how the six sources came into play. We've already talked about two of them—personal motivation and personal ability. Remember, we helped Kyler and others delay eating the marshmallow by adding distraction and distancing tactics to their existing personal motivation. And we saw results that would be quite a payoff for a more robust change plan.

The next two sources of influence that routinely act on you are equally easy to spot. The people who surround you both motivate and enable your habits. For instance, you may not want to quit smoking, but your life partner does, and that weighs heavily on your mind. Or perhaps co-workers keep handing you cigarettes and asking you to join them at break time. These powerful social forces add two more sources to our model of influence: *social motivation* and *social ability*.

Now for two rather subtle influences. If you remove human beings from the formula, the physical world that surrounds you still prods and enables you—for both good and evil. For instance, that refrigerator filled with soft drinks standing next to your exercise bike doesn't help you stick to your eating plan. The flashy ads on TV aren't exactly helping you stay on budget. The presence of a flat-screen TV in every room of your house positively distracts from your intention to finish your studies for a night class. But the ingenious new video game that requires you to jump around and swing a paddle has really helped with your exercise plan. You get the point. "Things" have an impact on what you do every day.

By combining these influences (we'll refer to them as *structural motivation* and *ability*) with personal and social forces, we have a full model of why you do what you do. These are the six hulking behemoths that either push *with* you or push *against* you.

BACK TO THE LAB

To see how these six sources actually work, let's return to the preteens who took part in the savings experiment. (To watch the experiment in action, visit ChangeAnything.com/exclusive.) The researchers manipulated all six sources in the following ways.

Source 1: Personal Motivation. First, we tapped into the subjects' existing desires and wants. After rank ordering the candies, the spending subjects were invited to taste their favorite treat. Yum. By contrast, the saving subjects were asked to think about something they really wanted to buy with their forty dollars. *Change Tactic:* If you interrupt your impulses by connecting with your goals during crucial moments, you can greatly improve your chances of success.

Source 2: Personal Ability. We next worked on personal ability by teaching savers how to keep a running total of how much they saved or spent on a sheet of paper. The savers all did this easily. The spenders, however, were taught no such technique, so their sinking net worth got lost in the rush to buy now. *Change Tactic:* Changing persistent and resistant habits always involves learning new skills.

Source 3: Social Motivation. Next, we made use of social forces. As the experiment unfolded, the spenders were joined by three other kids (confederates of our research team) who spent like there was no tomorrow—and encouraged the research subjects to join them. The savers were also joined by three confederates—but while two spent freely, the third said that she was trying to save and encouraged subjects to do the same. *Change Tactic:* Bad habits are almost always a social disease—if those around us model and encourage them, we'll almost always fall prey. Turn "accomplices" into "friends" and you can be two-thirds more likely to succeed.[5]

Source 4: Social Ability. Next we used confederates to *enable* good or bad choices. The savers were reminded by their "friend" that the prices in this store were outrageous and that if they could simply wait ten minutes they'd be able to get more for less elsewhere. Spenders received no such information. *Change Tactic:* Changing deeply entrenched habits invariably requires help, information, and real support from others. Get a coach, and you'll make change far more likely.

Source 5: Structural Motivation. Finally, we made use of *things*. Savers were paid in cold, hard cash. When they spent money, they had to fork over the real deal so they felt the loss at the very moment they made a purchase. Spenders, in contrast, were told their money was in an account. Their money was magically deducted from some abstract bucket. Thus, their spending felt painless— all gain, no pain—until they were in the car on the way home. *Change Tactic:* Directly link short-term rewards and punishments to the new habits you're trying to form, and you're far more likely to stay on track.

Source 6: Structural Ability. For the final source of influence, spenders walked into a room surrounded by tantalizing pictures of candy. Savers saw no such pictures in their room. *Change Tactic:* Small changes in your environment can have a surprising effect on your choices. For example, just add a few visual cues that help you focus on your goals, and your behavior will change rapidly.

THE BOY WHO COULD SEE

As this experiment so readily demonstrates, six sources of influence can and do profoundly affect behavior. When exposed to forces that both encouraged and enabled them to spend, the control group spent 68 percent of their earnings. (And remember, this spending frenzy happened within ten minutes of the subjects' solemnly declaring that they'd save most of their money.) When the same six sources were aimed at the savers—but this time encouraging and enabling them to save—they spent a mere 15 percent of their earnings.

But what would happen if someone caught a glimpse of what was going on behind the curtain? What if that person weren't blind to the forces that the research team was aiming at him or her? It turns out that one boy was able to do just that. His name was Isaac, and he saved thirty dollars—pretty much like everyone else in the saving group. But here's the difference: Isaac wasn't in the saving group. He was in the *spending* group. All six sources of influence were used to get him to spend his money—yet Isaac spent very little. Who was this kid, and what made him so invincible?

In order to figure out what made Isaac tick, we pored over the video evidence. We had recorded the whole experiment. In fact, you're welcome to watch Isaac in action at ChangeAnything.com/exclusive.

Without so much as a furrowed brow, Isaac used the six sources to his advantage. He controlled his motivation, used skills to enhance his ability, changed his social world, and manipulated his own physical environment. Here's how.

In the video, Isaac approached the store much more cautiously than did the other subjects in the spending group. While walking rather deliberately toward the place of temptation, Isaac told us later, he was thinking about the video game he intended to buy with his money after the experiment was over—trumping our team's attempt to influence him to spend now.

Next, Isaac employed a skill used by all savers—he calculated his bank balance in his head before making a buying decision. Nobody gave him a piece of paper, but it didn't matter to Isaac because he took advantage of his own personal ability by keeping a running total in his head.

You also can't help noting in the video that Isaac carefully distanced himself from the influence of the unhelpful accomplices. He looked slowly away and then stood apart. Isaac also stood at a much greater distance from the table than the other members of his research group—all of whom were drawn into the swirling vortex of retail doom.

As we continued our interview with Isaac, he summed up the premise of this book better than anyone had before. When asked how he saved so much money despite the fact that the researchers were doing everything in their power to get him to spend it, Isaac answered, in effect, "I could see what was happening, so I had to be careful."

So, exactly what does this experiment teach us? Overall, the six sources of influence had a huge impact on our subjects. When influenced to spend, they spent; when influenced to save, they saved. But not all subjects were equally affected. One young man saw what was happening and quite handily counteracted the effects. He wasn't blind, so he didn't stay outnumbered. And he didn't have to fail. He was in control of his choices because he was in control of the sources of influence that determined them. When asked why he had been successful, he didn't credit his moxie or stick-to-itiveness. In short, he escaped the willpower trap.

You gotta love Isaac. Better still, we all ought to *be* Isaac.

THE SCIENCE OF PERSONAL SUCCESS

In fact, that's the purpose of this book. We all need to learn how to intentionally do what people like Isaac do quite naturally. The difference between us and those who have succeeded at goals we struggle to achieve is not just willpower. It's that the achievers innately or consciously take steps to align these sources of influence in their favor. There is a science to personal success that allows us to be far more effective at creating the results we want than most of us even imagine.

Once we understand the forces that are acting on us, we no longer have to fall victim to them. We can knowingly design effective change plans. Our efforts won't have to feel so random and serendipitous. We can profoundly improve our ability to make changes in all areas of our life.

For example, we already saw how simply adding a little personal ability helped 50 percent more kids succeed at delaying gratification in the marshmallow experiment. As you'll see later, changing a few "accomplices" in your life into true "friends" adds more than 60 percent to the odds of success. And it gets better. To date we have looked into the details of personal change efforts of more than five thousand Changers—people around the globe who are taking on tough habits (in order to reduce their weight, advance a stalled career, shake an addiction, reverse a negative performance review, turn debt into wealth, and so forth). There are clear patterns for both success and failure in all of these attempts.

For example, in 2008 our Change Anything Labs published an important finding from this ongoing research in MIT's *Sloan Management Review*. Our discovery was the evidence that those who marshal

the six sources of influence in their change plan are *ten times* more likely to succeed than those who don't.

Now, there's a finding that will get and keep your attention. A thousand percent? As impressive as that statistic sounds, there is a bleak side to this discovery. Those who remain blind and outnumbered have almost no chance of success. What we describe in this book will help you understand what keeps you stuck and will equip you to engage the best of social science research to catapult you forward.

This book will help you learn to get the science of personal success working for you. Along the way, not only will you learn sound theory, but you'll also meet some of the fascinating Changers who have made it work for them.* For instance, Michael V. describes the influence strategies that enabled him to overcome decades of alcoholism and addiction. Melanie R. employs the same strategies to get her career out of performance-appraisal risk and onto the fast track. Patricia S. saves a failing marriage, and Michael E. loses weight and keeps it off for years. All succeed by using not one, two, or three, but six sources of influence—in combination. All have their eyes wide open. You don't hear them brag about their titanic will. You hear hard-earned insight about how they turned accomplices into friends, made use of the physical world, received training, and so forth. You'll hear how they escaped the willpower trap and created intentional change through deliberate application of solid science.

As you begin your study, we warn you that we have an agenda. Our goal isn't to write about change; it's to help create it.

---

* We refer to dozens of tactics used by Changers throughout the book. For simplicity, we take license at times to combine cases under one name rather than introduce multiple characters. In all cases, however, the tactics referenced have been used by and proven useful to real people facing real challenges.

What you hold in your hands is not just a book, but a portal. Your purchase of this book entitles you to access first-of-its-kind technology at ChangeAnything.com. Use the code on the inside of your book cover to access your free, limited time premium subscription to the site. So as you read, log on to gain access to some of the most advanced personal change tools social science can offer. To begin with, log on to simply enjoy a ringside view of the trials and triumphs of people just like you and to learn from their successes and setbacks. Then, chapter by chapter, develop a complete and practical plan for overcoming your personal challenges. Read on, log on, and move on by making change not only possible but inevitable.

Welcome to the science of personal success. Welcome to the power to change anything.

Be the Scientist
and the Subject

After reading the first chapter of this book, Tim F., a close friend of one of the authors, decided he'd apply the concepts to the challenge of losing weight. He realized that for years he had been sporadically using one or two weight-loss tactics (borrowed from any fad that promised easy and rapid success), but he had never put together a thoughtful plan. He most certainly hadn't used all six sources of influence—in combination. Tim also had never been able to lose weight and keep it off.

So this time Tim garnered advice from the strategy chapters that lie just ahead and applied an influence strategy to each of the six sources. For instance, to enhance his personal motivation, he worked hard to discover foods that were healthy—and that he also enjoyed eating. No more liver shakes and broccoli pudding. To improve his personal ability, he studied calorie counting. In his own words, "Without so much as consulting a chart, I can now tell you within ten calories how many I've eaten each day.

"I also attacked my social network," Tim continued. "My life partner was constantly filling our fridge with fatty foods and our pantry with sweets. Ironically, she was doing it for *me*—she didn't much care for those foods. So we talked and decided to surround ourselves with healthy food. I also asked her to celebrate with me each time I lost a pound. This helped keep me motivated."

After improving his social motivation and ability, Tim turned his attention to his reward structure. At first he couldn't think what to do to make eating a healthy diet more financially attractive, but then he read about the strategy of setting aside money for an organization he pretty much loathed, and then sending money to that very institution every time he failed to meet a monthly goal. Yikes!

"That got my attention," Tim explained. "I couldn't stand the thought of helping out a cause I despise."

Finally, Tim made use of his physical environment. He hung up posters, tracked and posted his weight loss, had his computer send upbeat reminders to his cell phone, and moved snacks to the basement storage room—so they wouldn't be so handy.

It was a great plan. But it didn't work. Okay, actually Tim lost a few pounds. But within a month he gave up and put all the weight back on. Plus five pounds. "I know the Change Anything approach works," he told us shortly after his setback. "It's just *me* that's the problem."

Tim was back in the willpower trap.

THIS ISN'T EASY

As you might suspect, when it comes to changing long-standing habits, Tim isn't alone in his struggle. When it comes to creating lasting change, failure is the rule, not the exception. Just take a look at the statistics:

- Marriage counseling works for fewer than one in five couples who use it.[1]
- A whopping 85 percent of us have had bosses who have tried—but failed—to get us to change in order to improve our performance.[2]
- Ninety-eight percent of us fail at keeping resolutions to change our bad habits.[3]
- Seventy percent of Americans who take out a home equity loan or other type of loan to pay off credit cards end up with the same (if not a higher) debt load within two years.[4]
- Only one in twenty dieters with a history of obesity is able to lose weight and keep it off for one or more years.[5]

So, what is the solution to Tim's problem? Where did he go wrong? Most people fail to reach their personal goals because they're in the dark about what's influencing their behavior. But Tim *wasn't* blind and outnumbered. He put together what he thought was a decent plan. He looked at all six sources of influence and came up with a tactic or two for each. So why did he stumble like most everyone else?

To answer this, consider a recent and rather intriguing piece of research.[6] A group of Stanford scholars examined the four most popular weight-loss programs in the United States to divine what works and what doesn't. Here's what they discovered:

1. All of the programs worked.
2. If people used them.
3. But people rarely used them.

That was Tim's problem. He had a plan—one that he liked quite a lot—but it worked for only a while. It didn't hold up to the test of time. So, what does it take to not only come up with a great change plan, but actually use it—forever?

YOU NEED TO STUDY YOU

Our Changers give us the answer. When you study people who not only succeed in changing but maintain their success for years, you'll quickly discover two things:

1. They stumbled as much as they succeeded.
2. Their change plan was homegrown.

The Changers we studied discovered what worked for them through a scientific process of trial and error. They didn't get it right the first time. In truth, when people are struggling with tenacious habits, few ever do. Instead, they took two steps forward and one step back—and sometimes the reverse. But they had a skillful way of learning from their setbacks so that their plan evolved in a deliberate direction. They snipped a little here and added a little there. They tried a new technique, observed, learned, and tried again. Day by day, week by week, they moved forward until one day their plan addressed all of their unique challenges—and they succeeded. Tailoring your personal change plan will require the same kind of purposeful experimentation.

So let's see how this scientific trial-and-error tactic might work for you. Let's say that, like Tim, you're trying to lose weight. That means that if you're going to succeed, you'll need to burn more calories (move around more) than you consume (eat somewhat differently). These are the obvious behavior changes you'll need to make.

Of course, a thousand people will offer advice about how to burn more and consume less. They'll suggest diet books, gym memberships, coaching services, pills, iPhone apps, and rent-a-chefs. And this is exactly where the plan breaks down. The advice well-intended colleagues eagerly impart may have been good for someone, somewhere, sometime, but it's unlikely to fit your peculiar needs. Researchers can tell you all about the science of weight loss (for example, a calorie is the energy it takes to heat one gram of pure water one degree centigrade at sea level), but nobody is ever going to be able to tell you what you personally need to do in order to master that bundle of nasty little calories glued to your belly.

What you need to succeed is not merely the science of weight loss; you need help from the *social* science of weight loss. That includes the study of you, living your unique life, in your particular environment, given your personal quirks.

Of course, nobody out there is studying *you*. Nobody else *can* study you. Researchers can give you generic hints that serve the broad population, but this type of advice serves only a small percentage of people a small percentage of the time. You're going to have to become a social scientist, using yourself as the subject. It's the only method that will withstand the test of time.

Talk to successful Changers you know, and you'll hear the same advice embedded in their stories of success. They'll tell you how in month one they discovered they had to stop going to lunch with the "Cholesterol Club" at work. In month four they realized that the jumbo box of Junior Mints in their drawer was more powerful than they were. In month eight they discovered that when they travel for business their plan falls apart. Bit by bit, they studied themselves like they were specimens under a microscope until they had a plan perfectly suited for the one subject they cared most about: *themselves.*

As troublesome as this recommendation may sound, what other choice do you have? Imagine how ludicrous it would be to expect career advice that helps a CFO who's been passed over for the CEO slot to also serve the needs of a shipping clerk who routinely receives passable reviews but is given no increase in pay. How likely would it be for the relationship advice that aids a newlywed couple to address the challenges of a middle-aged couple on the brink of divorce because of one partner's addictions?

Would you expect a diet that works for a sixty-year-old woman who struggles with depression and eats when she's unhappy to also work for a thirty-year-old man who has added twenty pounds since he started a sedentary job? Of course not. Both need to burn more calories than they eat. That we understand. But how they accomplish such a feat requires very different change plans.

So, if you want to succeed, you'll have to do what successful Changers do: You'll have to give up the hope of simply being the subject of some smart person's discovery. You'll have to be both scientist *and* subject—in search of the most important social science discovery of all: how to change *you*.

THE *SOCIAL* SCIENCE OF PERSONAL CHANGE

Good change scientists don't just thrash about trying every idea that makes the front cover of a popular magazine. Instead, they use a specialized form of scientific inquiry. Here's a quick overview of how Changers ensure that they stumble *forward* rather than *downward*.

First, examine when and where you currently give in to urges. This was Tim's first mistake. Rather than examining his unique challenges, he selected strategies that sounded new and interesting. Instead, he should have examined what we'll call his *crucial moments*—the times or circumstances in which his choices are the most consequential.

Tim was like the fellow who searched for his lost car keys under the streetlight near his car, not because he figured he dropped them there, but because he could see better under the light. Tim had selected convenient and cool-sounding influence methods, not relevant ones.

Once you've identified your specific vulnerabilities, create a personal change plan (or hypothesis). This plan consists of what you'll do to resist, remove, and even transform your urges during critical times.

Finally, implement the plan, observe the results, make changes in the plan (based on what worked and what didn't—resulting in a new plan), and repeat as needed until you've succeeded.

Let's see how this process works in practice, as demonstrated by

A.J.W., one of our intrepid Changers. Now, let's be clear. A.J. doesn't consider herself a social scientist. She's a thirty-one-year-old nurse, mother, and wife. But she did begin taking an interest in examining her own behavior after a rather startling incident.

A.J. was a two-pack-a-day smoker. The executives at the hospital where she works as a critical-care nurse frown on employees who drop ash on the patients they're resuscitating. So at key times throughout the day when A.J. could sneak a private moment and head out to the designated smoking area, she fumbled for a cigarette.

A.J. decided to quit smoking one day when she was called to help resuscitate a patient on the eighth floor of her hospital. At the time of the call she was on the first floor. Following hospital procedure, she bypassed the elevator (medical emergencies wait for no one) and hit the stairs. By the time she reached the third floor she was gasping for breath. When she arrived at the fourth she collapsed in a heap. Fortunately, other team members arrived on the eighth floor and saved the patient. But while A.J. sat burning with shame and gasping for breath on the concrete slab, she decided it was time to change.

SCIENTIFIC STRATEGY 1: IDENTIFY CRUCIAL MOMENTS

As A.J. thought about her challenge, she quickly realized that not all of her life moments were created equal. Most of the time she was busy, on autopilot, and not tempted to smoke. Well, not *that* tempted. The moments when she was simply dying for a smoke were actually fairly infrequent.

This is true for all of us and all of our bad habits. Not all of our life moments are equally challenging. For instance, few kids struggling with pornography addiction are tempted to indulge when their grandparents are in the room. Go figure. We don't lapse into lax work practices at the office when we know our work on a particular project is being used to evaluate whether we're fit for a promotion. We don't feel the urge to spend when we're balancing our checking account.

You get the point. When it comes to personal change, you don't have to be pushing yourself to the limit all the time. You need to focus on only a handful of moments when you're most at risk. We call these special circumstances crucial moments. These are the moments of truth that would lead to the results you want—if you could get yourself to enact the right behaviors.

A good way to look for crucial moments is to look for the conditions that create the greatest temptation for you. For example, you're tempted to ignore a customer request when it's out of the ordinary. You become cold and aloof with your life partner when you're under stress. You don't climb on the treadmill when you come down with a slight sniffle.

As you search for your own crucial moments, consider whether they come at certain *times*, in certain *places*, around certain *people*, or when you're in certain *physical* or *emotional* states. Different conditions affect different people differently. Only you can systematically search for the conditions of greatest importance to *your* change.

SCIENTIFIC STRATEGY 2: CREATE VITAL BEHAVIORS

Once you've identified your crucial moments, your next task is to create the rules you'll follow when temptation pays you a visit. Research shows that if you establish rules in advance of facing a challenge, you are far more likely to change your behavior when the crucial moment hits.[7] Instead of facing each instance as a unique event calling for a new choice, you've already decided what you'll do—and you're far more likely to comply.

When it comes to personal change, you'll want to set specific rules (not vague guidelines) that guide you to act in ways that eventually lead to what you want. That's why we call these essential actions *vital behaviors*. A vital behavior is any high-leverage action that will lead to the result you want. Crucial moments tell you when you're at risk. Vital behaviors tell you what to do.

To see how vital behaviors fit into a change plan, consider a rather fascinating study done by Peter Gollwitzer with twenty-one recovering heroin addicts who were desperately trying not only to stay clean but also to get jobs. Now, let's be clear about the challenge the subjects were facing. For a longtime heroin addict, the first forty-eight hours of withdrawal lead to muscle pains, cramps, perspiration outbreaks, freezing sensations, and diarrhea.

So, how did Gollwitzer help addicts to withstand these horrible withdrawal symptoms *and* get jobs? The addicts were encouraged to create résumés as a step toward securing employment. Imagine that. Create a résumé while powerful urges scream in your head.

After receiving résumé-writing instruction, subjects were given seven hours to complete the task. Half of the subjects jumped right into the assignment. The other half did one simple thing before they began: They identified crucial moments they'd face in the next seven hours *and* the vital behaviors they would enact when the moments struck.

For example, "When I feel sick [crucial moment], I will go to the bathroom but then return immediately to the task [vital behavior]."

The experimental subjects identified the physical state that could create a huge temptation for them and then planned the rule they'd follow to address it. The control subjects employed neither tactic.

The results from this groundbreaking study were remarkable. *None* of the first group of addicts succeeded at completing their résumés. But of those who prepared in advance for their crucial moments and vital behaviors, an astounding 80 percent succeeded.[8]

Back to A.J.

Now let's return to A.J. and see how identifying crucial moments and creating vital behaviors helped her with her smoking addiction. She started by examining circumstances that triggered her to smoke. Throughout much of the day she was working with patients—no problem there. In the mornings she was busy getting ready for her day and rarely lit up. Even lunch was pretty safe because she hung out with nonsmokers.

As A.J. thought about the conditions under which she was most likely to relapse, she concluded that she had two crucial moments. The first was at home when she was talking on the phone. The second was when she was driving to and from work. Both of these were times when she would mindlessly smoke.

So A.J. took a guess at two tailored (made-just-for-A.J.) vital behaviors. For several months she avoided using the phone as much as possible. She began using e-mail and texting in order to curtail long stretches on her cell phone. Second, she changed her driving route. She suspected that taking a new and unfamiliar route might help her be more mindful and less reactive.

Notice the *science* in A.J.'s plan. She created a hypothesis. That is, she made a calculated guess about both her crucial moments and her vital behaviors. Then came the social science. Rather than following Tim's example and simply grabbing the latest fad, she based her plan on her own unique circumstances.

Of course, A.J. didn't pin all her hopes on her first plan. Instead, she conducted a full-on personal experiment. She identified her crucial moments, created and tried her vital behaviors, saw what worked and what didn't, made adjustments, and repeated the process as needed.

SCIENTIFIC STRATEGY 3: ENGAGE ALL SIX SOURCES OF INFLUENCE

So, let's say you have concluded that in order to turn around a mediocre performance review, your crucial moment is at the end of high-visibility projects. You tend to give short shrift to formalities such as presentations, project reviews, and reports. You've always told yourself that you value substance over style. Now you realize that this philosophy has cost you. You need to demonstrate your substance by practicing a new vital behavior. You're going to add two polishing steps to every critical document you prepare.

Your next problem is getting yourself to actually do that—no small task. It's four thirty p.m. on a Friday and you're exhausted. You're about to push Send on a document that you just typed up in a rush. The old voice is saying, "Why should I have to spend two more hours just to perfume this?"

Now it's time to move from thinking to doing.

Having identified your crucial moments and vital behaviors, you now have to develop a change plan to get yourself to recognize those moments and engage in those behaviors.

But how?

In "Escape the Willpower Trap" we answered this question. The only reasonable way to battle the wide world out there, which is so perfectly organized to keep you making the same mistakes, is to use all six sources of influence in combination. Here's a sample of how this might work.

Once Again, Back to A.J.

A.J. discovered that the reason she couldn't quit smoking was that all six sources of influence were working against her. Over time, she recruited all of them to her side. Here's how.

Personal Motivation. First of all, A.J. developed wise tactics to increase her motivation to stick with her vital behaviors. For example, in her crucial moments she would conjure images she was privy to as a respiratory therapist. She had watched patients literally suffocate to death due to symptoms of smoking-related diseases. When the smoking hunger settled on her, she was able to consider her *default future* (See the chapter "Source 1: Love What You Hate") by recalling these incidents and the reactions of patients' family members after their loss. Likewise, she found that posting inspiring quotes on her mirror to use as conscious pep talks when she was feeling weak helped her at key times. But she soon came to realize that motivation strategies like these weren't enough. Her problem had not been just a lack of motivation. She had ability challenges as well.

Personal Ability. Ultimately A.J. realized that she needed to learn a great deal more about behavior modification. Her reading led her to focus on developing distraction strategies to increase her *will skill* (we cover this in the chapter "Source 2: Do What You Can't"). Her challenge during crucial moments was that her hand wanted to do something with her mouth. That familiar motion was soothing to her. So she distracted herself with straws. When her hand involuntarily traveled toward her mouth, she grabbed a straw and placed that in her mouth instead of a cigarette. In fact, she'd even take a long drag on the straw, which she found to be a good breathing and relaxation tactic!

A.J. realized she also needed new skills to help her create new habits. She loved to read—so she scoured books to gather tips that would help her. She learned, for example, that she needed more

	MOTIVATION	ABILITY
PERSONAL	1	2
SOCIAL	3	4
STRUCTURAL	5	6

skills in distinguishing her own emotions. She discovered that smoking was as much a psychological as a physiological addiction. Over time she began to pay more attention to signals of stress, and she deliberately practiced skills (more on this in the chapter "Source 2: Do What You Can't") to calm and focus herself—which made the compulsion to smoke much easier to handle.

Social Motivation and Ability. Next A.J. turned to her social network, where she transformed some accomplices (people who encouraged her to smoke) into friends (they now encouraged her to quit) by conducting a *transformation conversation* (which we discuss in the chapter "Sources 3 and 4: Turn Accomplices into Friends").

Structural Motivation. Kicking the smoking habit had a built-in structural motivation. A.J. smoked two packs a day and her husband smoked one. Each pack cost $4.50. That added up to about $400 a month they were spending on cigarettes! A.J. explains, "The cost of smoking was a huge driver to quit. When we finally kicked the habit we experienced a real positive change in our financial way of life."

Structural Ability. Finally, A.J. changed her physical environment. She altered the way she drove to work and tried to avoid other physical locations that triggered her thoughts of lighting up. Similarly, she removed all ashtrays from her home to jar her into remembrance of her decision to quit in case she started mindlessly looking for a cigarette.

These are just a sampling of some of the influence tactics A.J. employed as she studied herself and learned what she needed to do in order to stop smoking forever. They were a starting point for her—not the final destination. She had tried and failed to quit before. This time she committed herself to being a scientist and not just a subject. That meant that she would see setbacks as information, and she would use that information to improve her change plan rather than blaming herself when she experienced them.

SCIENTIFIC STRATEGY 4: TURN BAD DAYS INTO GOOD DATA

Did A.J. correctly identify all of her crucial moments and vital behaviors—from day one? Did she nail the six sources she needed to get her to do her vital behaviors? No.

Just like the rest of us, A.J. had to learn what was working for her and what wasn't and then make adjustments. For instance, she soon began to see unanticipated sources of influence that conspired against her. Unfortunately, one of them was her father. Every Saturday she and her husband would have supper with her dad—a legendary chain smoker himself. Being around him, in his house, and in this familiar smoking setting was overwhelmingly difficult for A.J.

But instead of smoking with her father and then feeling bad and quitting her change effort, she noted what happened in the company of her father and then used the information to her advantage. She updated her change plan. She started by minimizing her visits to her dad's house, and then she tried her best to visit with him in safer settings. By revising her change plan, A.J. turned a bad day into good data.

It's important to comprehend this adjusting process, because no matter how brilliant your initial change plan is, if you're dealing with long-standing habits, your plan won't work. Okay, it might work for a while, but sooner or later a crucial moment will hit and you'll unceremoniously give in to the temptation. You'll have a bad day.

This is the moment your real test begins. In the face of what feels like abject failure, you'll become either depressed or curious. You'll become depressed if you blame yourself, become discouraged, and fall into a total binge—only making matters worse and lowering your self-esteem. If you become curious, you'll step back and examine the data, *learn* from what just happened, and then *adjust* the plan. So, there's your choice. You can bump into a new barrier and become depressed and quit, or you can experience the very same setback, become curious, and *turn a bad day into good data*.

APPLYING THE SCIENCE OF CHANGE TO WORK

We've looked at smoking and weight loss, but how might these four scientific strategies help you solve a problem at work? Say you're trying to get unstuck in your career. How might you develop, test, and alter a personal change plan to your benefit?

1. Identify Crucial Moments. You start by scanning your typical day on the job and realize that your biggest barrier to being viewed as a key player at work is that you're constantly getting sidetracked with tasks that aren't very important to the company's success. Your primary assignment is essential to the organization's success, but you also fill your time with tangential tasks that often keep you off target. So you ask yourself, "What are the crucial moments that keep me from focusing on my primary assignment?" You soon realize that your biggest challenge comes when a co-worker asks you to take on a new task and you worry about saying no. You don't want to disappoint anyone. This is your crucial moment: Someone is asking you to take on a task and you feel obligated to say yes.

2. Create Vital Behaviors. Next you think about a possible tailor-made vital behavior. What actions will you need to take in this crucial moment? You talk to friends, study what others do who don't seem to struggle with always saying yes, and conclude that your vital behavior is: *Never make a commitment in the moment. Promise to consider the request and respond within twenty-four hours.* This vital behavior will become the rule you'll follow. You won't decide upon it each time; you'll merely implement it.

3. Engage All Six Sources of Influence. For example, get started by approaching the most obvious sources: Knowing that you're bad at saying no, you decide to bolster your skills. You take an assertiveness class and read up on the topic. Plus you share your problem with your boss, who promises to support your efforts to stay focused on high-yield tasks. You now feel prepared.

4. Turn Bad Days into Good Data. For two weeks you stay on task. You do agree to an occasional side job, but only when it makes strategic sense and when you've got a slight lag in your own schedule. Then one day someone asks for help on a tangential task—and suggests that his boss would be pleased if you helped. In fact, he implies that you'll be seen in a bad light if you don't lend a hand. So you agree and then fall behind with your own critical work. At first you beat yourself up for caving in to a sidetracking request, but then you remember that the better response is to take corrective action. Next time, when an authority figure asks you to take an assignment, you'll get more social support (social ability) for your vital behavior by routing that person through your own boss, who can then make the choice. You turn a bad day into good data, keep with your plan, make an occasional adjustment, and eventually improve your performance review.

So now we know what to tell our friend Tim, who's trying to lose weight. The good news is that he realized that he needed to bring several influences to bear—in unison—when facing his weight-loss challenge. But he missed out on an important part of the scientific process. If he expects to succeed in the future, he also needs to create a plan that's based on his idiosyncratic challenges, not on the latest fad or the recommendation of an enthusiastic friend. Then, as both scientist and subject, he needs to implement the plan, study the results, turn a bad day into good data, and continue doing so until every last challenge is met. That's how problems that appear impossible transform into solutions that are inevitable.

START TAKING NOTES

While we're exploring the science of personal change, let's examine one of the most important scientific tools you own: *a pencil (or the electronic equivalent, a keyboard)*.

How might these humble instruments play a significant role in your change effort? You might be surprised. Consider the following rather startling discovery. A team of researchers from New York University worked with students whose grades suffered because they procrastinated studying. They gave half of the procrastinators information on how to improve their study habits. The other half were given the same information—plus pencil and paper. They were told, "Decide now where and at what times you will study in the next week, and *write it down*."

Those who recorded their plan studied more than twice as many hours as those who didn't.[9] Repeated studies show that simply writing down a plan increases your chance of success by more than 30 percent.[10]

So start now. Grab a piece of paper to record your off-the-top-of-your-head thoughts about your crucial moments. Then make your best guess about the vital behaviors that will serve you best in these moments. Better yet, activate your complimentary subscription at ChangeAnything.com using the code found inside your book cover, where you can make electronic notes.

Also, as you read the next five chapters, write down your plan for engaging all six sources of influence. Then learn what's working and what isn't, and make adjustments. If you keep a record of your evolving plan, you'll make new mistakes rather than repeating the old ones. The goal here is not perfection, but progress. By actually recording your plans, you will increase your ability to follow through, enhance your motivation to change, and expand your capacity to learn and adjust along the way.

PART II

THE SIX SOURCES OF INFLUENCE

Source 1

Love What You Hate

By now it should be abundantly clear that when it comes to changing ourselves, it's best to use strategies from each of the six sources of influence—especially those that are currently working against us. If we don't, we're going to be outnumbered and out of luck. So to help facilitate this tactic, we'll jump right into Source 1, *personal motivation*, and see what it has to offer a fledgling Changer.

When it comes to changing ourselves, here's the biggest challenge: The things we *should* do are often boring, uncomfortable, or even painful. Ergo, we don't want to do them. Well, that's not completely accurate. We do want to do them—in the abstract, just not in real life. We want to do them in the future, just not in the present.

For instance, when psychologist Daniel Read asked subjects to make out a shopping list, he found that if they were shopping for what they'd eat *right now*, 74 percent picked tempting chocolate over healthy fruit.

No big surprise there. But if he asked them to pick what they would eat *a week from now*, 70 percent chose the fruit.[1] Someday we want to do the right thing.

Taking our cue from Read's subjects, we too have plans for changing—tomorrow. We're going to get up early, eat healthy fruit while shunning chocolate, exercise vigorously, study abstruse but important journal articles that will enhance our careers, and stop losing our temper. That's right, tomorrow we're going to be a force to be reckoned with.

None of this tomorrow talk would be necessary if we could find a way to enjoy doing the right thing today. We're good at doing what we enjoy. If only we enjoyed doing what is good for us, we wouldn't have to *resist* our short-term impulses (never easy); nor would we have to *remove* those impulses altogether (sometimes impossible). If we could only *convert* our dislikes into likes, we'd be unstoppable.

But is it even possible to love what you hate?

THERE ARE PEOPLE WHO LOVE WHAT YOU HATE

To see how people find a way to love what most people would most certainly hate, let's visit a sprawling garden located across Guanabara Bay from the city of Rio de Janeiro. There we find Valter dos Santos talking excitedly about the work he and his colleagues do every day. As you listen to Valter discuss his job, you can't help noticing that he sounds more like a public relations executive than an hourly employee.

He starts out, "I have been a picker here for twenty-six years. I am proud to be a picker."

Valter goes on to enthuse about living at the center of the green movement, where he and his co-workers do some of the most important work imaginable.

Then Valter carefully puts on a pair of tattered gloves, scurries over to a mammoth garbage dump, and picks through some of the foulest-smelling trash in the world. Valter is a *catadore*—or picker. He, along with two thousand other *catadores*, extracts recyclable material at Gramacho Garden—one of the world's largest dumps. Despite working conditions that would choke a maggot, Valter and his colleagues take great pride, even pleasure, in their work.[2]

COULD *YOU* LOVE WHAT YOU HATE?

Valter and his co-workers have found a way to take satisfaction from a task that would disgust most human beings. But how? More to the point, since resolving our own bad habits often calls for us to do something we find noxious, tedious, or stressful, what if we could react to it as the *catadores* do?

It turns out that we can. Consider one of our Changers, Louie C. After a decade of suffering from a crippling shopping addiction, Louie eventually overcame his burning desire to buy every new gadget in sight. This was no mean feat considering the fact that at home, at work, and at play, Louie was surfing the Net for deals. At one point he logged more than a quarter of a million dollars in debt and went through bankruptcy; at his lowest point, he sold his mother's car to raise money to buy a moose head for his den.

How did Louie turn his life around? When the police showed up at Louie's doorstep (at his mother's request) and the judge gave him the choice of prison or counseling, Louie decided that it was time to change.

Like the rest of the Changers, Louie's turnaround called for a variety of strategies, but one came from a surprising source. Louie learned to take pleasure from what he once loathed. Here's how he described the turnaround.

"I didn't think it could ever happen," Louie explained. "It makes me cringe now to think of how I used to lose control of my spending. And the strangest thing is, I now get a bit of a rush out of seeing my net worth grow. I feel like a different person. Now when I'm tempted to make an impulse purchase, I take pleasure in knowing that I'm no longer selling out my future in order to buy the gadget of the moment."

SEE, FEEL, AND BELIEVE IN THE FUTURE

As you listen closely to Louie, you'll note that one of the secrets to enjoying an activity that isn't yet hardwired into the pleasure center lies in our ability to see, feel, and believe in the future it will bring us. It's possible to diminish the immediate pleasure of a bad habit by connecting it to the pain it will eventually cause us. Similarly, by contemplating the pleasure a good habit will eventually yield, we can make the habit itself more enjoyable. The good news is that when we do take the effort to consider the long-term effects of our actions, we can overcome our hardwired short-term bias. Thinking differently actually rewires the brain.[3]

Unfortunately, for most of us it's hard to get that rewiring started in the first place because it's so enormously difficult to keep our future in mind in light of the fact that our present is always so real, compelling, and in our face. That's why human beings are so notoriously myopic. We know how the delicious chocolate will taste right *now*, but we fail to feel any of the effects our chocolate choice will yield in the future. In the heat of an argument with our life partner, we know how wonderful it feels to take a cheap shot, but our future—the way it *could* feel if we swallow our pride and apologize—is typically out of mind and therefore offers no motivation in the moment.

At work, when the boss asks us if an insane decision he has just presented to the team makes sense, we know what it will feel like to disagree with him in public (we've taken more than our fair share of ugly stares and put-downs), so we aren't exactly thinking about what it will feel like to live with the stupid decision later on.

In short, when faced with the choice of enjoying now or paying later, we often think only about the now. This means that when deciding if we want to serve our short-term interests, we must take steps to see, feel, and believe in the future we'll face if we continue to satisfy our urges. Here are five tactics for turning our future into an ally for change.

TACTIC 1: VISIT YOUR DEFAULT FUTURE

Every eight seconds a baby boomer in America turns sixty-five, and more than half of them will be armed during their retirement with little more than their social security stipend and thinning hair. A majority of forty-five-year-old Americans have less than fifty thousand dollars saved for retirement.[4] Many of them are dooming their golden years to a period of financial struggle because they've refused to contemplate what will actually happen to them when they stop receiving a paycheck. They haven't merely lived in denial; they've lived in carefully crafted ignorance.

If you're facing a similar fate because you're having a hard time motivating yourself to make short-term sacrifices, there is a cure. *Visit your default future*—today. Your default future is the life you'll live if you continue behaving as you currently are. It's the life that's hurtling toward you—but you aren't motivated by it because you aren't currently in it.

With a little imagination you can pull that unpleasant future forward and wire it into your current decision making. One powerful way to do this is to take a field trip to your future. An actual experience like this can profoundly reshape your feelings about your choices when the pep talks and guilt trips you've tried in the past have had no effect.

For instance, when it comes to your finances, think back to a visit you recently may have made to an acquaintance who is currently living on nothing more than social security and is suffering as a result. That could be you. Or calculate what you will have to live on after retirement if you continue your current spending and saving patterns—and then try to live on that much for a month. Visit your future self: Taste your future meal, lounge in your future furniture, and sit in your future car. The experience just may change your life.

Our inability to see our future is particularly troubling when certain aspects aren't guaranteed to happen—but will have cataclysmic consequences if they do. Under these circumstances, it can be even more important to personally examine what might happen to you—on a bad day.

Consider Jacob L., another one of our Changers. During his early twenties he was seriously addicted to Internet pornography, often spending most of his free time and much of his disposable income on the habit.

"I figured no harm could come from it," Jacob explained, "until one day at work I was jolted to my senses when I spotted a co-worker and friend (who was also a big pornography fan) being escorted out of the building in handcuffs. It turns out he had taken secret photos of his next-door neighbor's daughter in various states of undress and loaded them onto his computer. When he accidentally brought one of the photos to his laptop screen in a meeting, he was busted and hauled off to jail.

"It was horrible," Jacob continued. "Even though I hadn't done anything like that, those handcuffs felt like my handcuffs. It was as if I had been given a privileged view into my likely future, and the warning hit me hard."

Glimpses into worst-case scenarios often propel people to change—in all kinds of areas of their life, not just addictions. Consider bike riding—a healthy habit. But what if you ride without a helmet? The odds are that nothing serious will happen to you. But then there's the unlikely but horrible head injury. So, given the low likelihood of a head injury, who is most likely to go to the inconvenience of wearing a helmet (and the loss of feeling the wind in their hair)?

To answer this question, one of the authors talked to his neighbor—an emergency room nurse—inquiring how many emergency room employees wear helmets when riding bikes or motorcycles.

"We all do!" she exclaimed. "We work in an *emergency room*. We see firsthand what happens to bikers when they're hit by a car or truck. It's often lethal. That's why we call motorcycles 'donor cycles.' People without helmets crash and destroy their brains, and we then harvest the rest of their organs for transplants."

Obviously, these emergency room workers *feel* differently about wearing helmets than much of the public does because they have different *experiences.* They see where an unsafe practice just might lead them. When it comes to our own unsafe, unhealthy, and troublesome habits, we need to shine a light on reasonably possible worst-case scenarios before we experience them. Instead of purposely ignoring the data, we need to bring it to the forefront of our minds now, where it can help propel us in the right direction before it's too late. Creating a tangible way for you to visit your default future is a powerful way to do that.

TACTIC 2: TELL THE WHOLE VIVID STORY

Many of us have already taken a peek into our future and know all too well what will happen to us if we continue down our current, unhealthy path. We just don't feel it. And the reason we don't feel it is that we play mental tricks with ourselves to keep from doing so. We think only about the partial and convenient truth. For example, we say "might" even though we know the truth is "most certainly." We assume that our fate will follow luck rather than natural law. Mostly, we distract our attention from the default future by filling our mind with the present experience. In short, we nurture massive gaps in the truth—rather than fill in the ugly details.

Changers know better. When facing temptations, they take great care to tell themselves the whole story. Consider Michael V., an alcoholic ex-con and one of our amazing Changers. Michael started drinking at a young age and moved quickly from drinking to drugs and from drugs to crime—to pay for his addiction. After several years of breaking and entering, theft, and addiction, Michael lost his wife, his family, most of his friends, all of his possessions, and eventually his freedom—ending up in prison.

As we'll see throughout the remainder of this book, Michael used influence strategies from each of the six sources to get back his life. When it comes to Source 1, personal motivation, Michael explained how creating a habit of *telling the whole vivid story* works to his benefit.

"When I'm watching TV, an advertisement will come on showing a group of people enjoying a martini at a piano bar. To this day that commercial can get my thoughts heading in a dangerous direction. My natural inclination is to start thinking 'I can do that.' Sure, I'm a recovering alcoholic, but why not enjoy a social drink with friends? What harm can that be?

"But that's not *my* story, nor is it *the whole* story. My story plays out differently. If I join the group at the piano bar, I'll drink the martini. Then I'll be back tomorrow. Then I'll shift to hard liquor, I'll soon be on a binge, and one day I'll wake up lying in my own vomit or maybe even in jail. And by the way, that's not merely what *might* happen to me. That's what *will* happen to me."

You'll notice that when telling the story, Michael doesn't merely tell the whole story; he also uses rather vivid language. Instead of suggesting that a drink would be bad for him, he describes potential consequences in vibrant detail. The power of Michael's labeling tactic isn't something known just to him; it's actually based on solid science. For instance, ongoing research is showing that subjects who set aside money for generic "long-term savings" are less faithful in making their monthly contributions than those who choose to create a "New Roof" account.[5] Specific and meaningful labels identify specific consequences and as such are more motivating than watered-down generic terms.

So, as you tell your whole story, use vibrant language. Replace innocuous terms such as "unhealthy" and "problematic" with poignant terms such as "bankrupt," "fired," "divorced," and "emphysema." Stop comforting yourself with fairy tales, innocent language, and half-truths.

Use the same type of poignant and vivid language when portraying what will happen when you do the right thing. For instance, you're not merely going to be healthy; you're going to play with your grandkids on the floor. You won't just have more money for your retirement; you'll cruise the Mediterranean. When considering both healthy and unhealthy actions, you deserve the whole truth, the vivid truth, and nothing but the truth.

TACTIC 3: USE "VALUE WORDS"

For this next tactic we pay a quick visit to one of the most fascinating restaurants and rehab centers on earth—Delancey Street in San Francisco, California. It is there that we find Mimi Silbert, the founder and genius behind the most successful life-changing facility on earth. The entire facility is run by Mimi and fifteen hundred residents—each with an average of eighteen felony convictions. Delancey Street admits drug addicts and criminals and transforms more than 90 percent of them into productive citizens.

With a near-perfect record in a field in which a 5 percent success rate is common, you can bet that Dr. Silbert relies on all six sources of influence to work her magic. When it comes to learning to love what you hate, Mimi explains how she teaches former drug dealers, thieves, gang leaders, and prostitutes to link their actions to their values.

"We talk about values all the time. Even when we're teaching a new resident how to set the table while he's withdrawing from crack cocaine, we don't just talk about knives and forks; we talk about pride. We talk about showing respect for those who will sit at this place at the table. You're not just setting a table; you're working as part of a team. You're carrying your fair share of the work. You're not letting people down. You're becoming trustworthy. It's values, values, values—all the time."

What Mimi is explaining here isn't merely a matter of semantics. It's about keeping in mind some of the more important reasons behind your current actions and sacrifices. For instance, the Brazilian *catadores* at Gramacho Garden derive pleasure from their job, not by focusing on the disgusting elements of sorting garbage but by connecting their activities to their values. In their words, they're helping save the planet. In a world full of polluters, they're "green masters."

You can enjoy the same benefits with your own personal challenges. Stop obsessing over the unpleasant aspects of what you're required to do, and focus your attention on the values you're supporting. The words you use to describe what you're doing profoundly affect your experience of the crucial moment. For instance, when sticking to a lower-calorie diet, don't undermine your own motivation by describing your choices as "starving" or "going without." You're doing far more than manipulating calories. You're becoming healthy; you're sticking to your promise; you're sacrificing so that you'll be mobile when playing with your grandkids. This difference in description may sound small, but words matter. They focus the brain on either the positive or negative aspects of what you're doing.

An interesting example of the power of value labels comes from

Stanford psychologist Lee Ross. He had subjects play a game in which they could either cooperate or compete. In each round, subjects had to decide whether to share money with others or keep it for themselves. Half the subjects were told it was the "Community Game." It was introduced to the other half as the "Wall Street Game." Both groups played exactly the same game, but the second group was far more likely to steal, lie, and cheat. By connecting their actions to their image of "Wall Street," subjects (and this is truly unfortunate) felt more comfortable behaving like scoundrels and feeling good about it. In contrast, those who used the word "community" felt fine about winding up with less money because they were sacrificing for the "common good."[6]

Learn from Drs. Silbert and Ross. Carefully choose the words you'll use to describe your vital behaviors. You aren't merely going without your favorite goodies; you're keeping a promise to yourself. You aren't simply climbing stairs; you're choosing health. In short, you're supporting your values—and that thought can be very satisfying.

TACTIC 4: MAKE IT A GAME

Next we take a trip to New Zealand and look in on two teams of thirteen bruising men as they push and kick each other to gain control of a leather ball. What exactly are these people doing? They're engaging in the sport of rugby—and they're doing it for *fun*. They're enjoying themselves because they've transformed smacking one another into a contest with winners and losers, posted scores, uniforms, and prizes.

When facing a personal challenge, many successful Changers increase their personal motivation by turning chores into games. A *game* has three important design elements:

1. Limited time.
2. A small challenge.
3. A score.

For instance, Changer Peter K., finally completed his doctoral thesis by turning it into a game. For years he had procrastinated writing the 180-page tome that would be his dissertation. Threats from his adviser, a pending promotion that required the final document, and pleading from his loved ones couldn't get Peter to step up to the daunting task.

But then one day, Peter made it all a game. First, he gave himself ninety days to finish. Tasks turn into games when you're racing against a clock. Next, Peter broke the ninety days into one-day increments. Each day he would produce two pages.

"Two pages I could do standing on my head," Peter explained.

By sizing the challenge to his current level of motivation, Peter increased the likelihood he'd take action. Each day would be a "win" if he merely finished two pages. Breaking the goal into smaller chunks was enormously motivating to Peter, as it gave him ninety triumphs along the way rather than only one big success at the end.

Next, Peter took a picture of himself in borrowed doctoral robes. Then he cut the photo into ninety pieces. Each day as Peter finished his pages he would add one block of his mosaic to a chart in his bedroom. Three weeks into his game, Peter reported bashfully, "I'm embarrassed to admit how happy it made me feel to simply glue a piece of my picture onto the chart. It was the biggest thrill of my day."

By breaking his goal into small wins, setting a limited time frame, and developing a meaningful way of keeping score, Peter turned something noxious into something surprisingly motivating by making it fun. After he received his PhD, his employer gave him a ten-thousand-dollar-per-year raise. Now *that's* fun.

It's hard to overstate how much easier it is to love what you hate when you turn a tough task into a game. Another compelling example of learning to love what you hate comes from young diabetics. Imagine how hard it would be to get a newly diagnosed eleven-year-old to give herself six painful shots per day. Who could love a shot? Fortunately, the vast majority of kids today manage to follow this regimen just fine because the goal of long-term management has been turned into a game.

Several times a day, kids put a drop of blood on a meter that gives them a "score." They know they're winning if their score is between 60 and 120—a healthy blood-sugar reading. So now they're playing a game. They have a limited time frame (every couple of hours); a small challenge (stay between 60 and 120); and a score (the current reading).

These three elements turn the drudgery of worrying about one's long-term health into an engrossing and motivating game. We're not suggesting that diabetic kids prefer the testing game to an hour on their Wii—but their experience of the process of diabetes management changes profoundly when it's broken down in this way.[7] It also transforms something far-off and fuzzy (health management) into something short-term and in control. By focusing on the short term and turning the task into a game, far more diabetic kids are now succeeding in the long term by living long and healthy lives.

TACTIC 5: CREATE A PERSONAL MOTIVATION STATEMENT

Consider the experience of the rather remarkable Changer Rosemary C. She escaped a life of prostitution, drug dealing, and heroin addiction by transforming into a healthy, nonaddicted citizen. She did it by relying heavily on, of all things, a simple statement she would review whenever temptations overpowered her. By reciting her simple but personally powerful statement, Rosemary caught a glimpse of this person—the healthy, nonaddicted version of herself—and pulled that vision to the forefront of her mind every time she faced a temptation.

It all started when Rosemary courageously left the streets behind and secured a clerical job working for a woman she deeply admired. One day Rosemary completed a difficult assignment a bit early and proudly gave it to her boss. As she turned to leave, her boss looked at the polished assignment, looked back at Rosemary, and said, "Thank you for being so dependable."

"Dependable"? No one had ever called her dependable before. She had never seen herself that way either. She had been described as a hooker or a dealer or an addict, but never dependable.

That word became Rosemary's anchor. Over the next two years, during crucial moments when she was tempted to give up on her aspirations, she promised herself that before she made a choice, she would recite a brief statement that said, "I am not a hooker. I am not a dealer. I am not an addict. I am the kind of person others can depend on." It was nothing eloquent. But it shook Rosemary's insides most times when she recited it. And it created a seismic shift in her feelings about the choice she faced. Her temptations seemed less interesting. Doing the right things seemed a little more satisfying.

Where is Rosemary today? She has just earned her bachelor's degree. Now, that's pretty dependable.

So, as you're doing your best to stay on the right path, remember Rosemary. As you face crucial moments during which you must decide whether to stick to your exercise plan, hold tight to your budget, get up each morning and hit the books to advance in your career, or otherwise do something challenging, use the power of a Personal Motivation Statement to rewire your thoughts about your choice.

A good statement can include references to your default future. It can tell the whole vivid story that you might otherwise ignore in these moments. And it should be laden with value words.[8] One of the simplest ways to create a first draft of a Personal Motivation Statement is to have a trusted friend conduct a *motivational interview* with you. This is a handy but powerful process that starts with a simple structured conversation.

To see how powerful this special conversation can be, let's go back to the emergency room for a moment. But this time we're not talking helmets and organ transplants. Instead we're face-to-face with an inebriated fourteen-year-old.

You're treating a young man who passed out after an all-night drinking binge. To make matters worse, the boy was drinking *alone*—a foreboding sign that he's at risk for alcoholism. And you're not a social worker; you're a nurse. The boy has now sobered up, and his parents are waiting to take him home. You've got fifteen to twenty minutes to do *something* to help him find some motivation to change—a hopelessly short amount of time for what seems like a serious problem.

Recent studies had emergency room professionals conduct motivational interviews with the patients in similar circumstances, and discovered that this brief chat can have a powerful effect. There is overwhelming evidence that those who benefit from one are significantly more likely to change—long after the emergency room conversation ends.[9]

After treating the patients' injuries, caregivers conducted a fifteen- to twenty-minute interview wherein they asked injured abusers to discuss the future they'd like to live, how they were going to get there, and so forth. In the end, subjects crafted a powerful statement of their default and desired futures along with a few thoughts about their plan to get what they wanted. When the subjects are allowed to envision for themselves what lies ahead if they do and don't change (even if only for a few minutes), many make profound improvements in their lives.

You can access a basic agenda for a motivational interview at ChangeAnything.com/exclusive.

SUMMARY: LOVE WHAT YOU HATE

As you work on your change effort, rid yourself of the notion that success will require a lifetime of self-denial. You can take steps to change how you feel about both negative *and* positive choices by making your likely future salient, poignant, and real. You can learn to love what you hate. To do so, keep the following tactics in mind.

Visit Your Default Future. Is there a way to get a clear view of your most likely future? Visit someone or someplace that is pretty close to where you're heading. The more vivid you make the visit, the more powerfully it can influence you.

Tell the Whole Vivid Story. What are the specific descriptive words that sum up where you are or where you're heading?

Use Value Words. You know the sacrifice you'll be making—but *why* are you doing it? What principle are you adhering to? What quality are you developing? What standard are you adhering to?

Make It a Game. Is there a way you can set a time frame or small milestones along the way to achieving your greater goal? Is there someone you can compete with for encouragement?

Create a Personal Motivation Statement. Reconnect yourself to your reasons for changing during crucial moments by preparing a Personal Motivation Statement. Draw on your default future. Tell the whole vivid story. Use value words in a concise way that will change how you feel when you most need to.

NEXT STEPS

Review each of the five tactics and decide which best suit your needs. Build one or more into your written change plan, or use the Ideas Engine located at ChangeAnything.com. Since all Source 1 tactics deal with how you *think about* both the future and the present, they're only a thought away. That makes them immediately available and totally under your control. Source 1 can be a wonderful ally.

However, don't forget: We've examined only one source of influence so far. When used in isolation, one tactic is likely to be insufficient to either motivate or enable change. So, keep reading. Learn tactics from each of the six sources and then carefully apply them in combination. There's no need to show up at a gunfight with only a Nerf gun.

Finally, if you'd like additional Source 1 tactics or tactics that are designed specifically for your personal challenge, go to ChangeAnything. com/exclusive. There you'll find hints, articles, video clips, connections to people who are making similar changes, and a whole host of other tools for helping you use Source 1 to love what you hate.

Source 2

Do What You Can't

	MOTIVATION	ABILITY
PERSONAL	1	2
SOCIAL	3	4
STRUCTURAL	5	6

Think back to a time when you were making progress toward a personal goal, but then you fell off the wagon. How did you feel about yourself the next day? If you're like most of us, you felt miserable. But your disappointment probably didn't last very long because if you're a normal human being, you picked yourself up, dusted yourself off, and then blamed yourself for being a wimp because you didn't have the personal motivation to follow through with your plan.

Now, why would anyone point the finger of blame at their *own* lack of motivation? Because it seems valid. Consider your last setback. You faced temptation, and temptation won. Your life partner did something insensitive, and a fully formed sarcastic comment presented itself to your brain. Then it began traveling involuntarily down a series of neurons toward your mouth. You had a moment of hesitation in which you thought better of taking a cheap shot—but only a moment. And you let your lips fly. If you had only held firm, you wouldn't have suffered the subsequent two-day cold war. So, what is there to blame besides your lack of willpower?

Actually, lots. There are at least five other forces acting on you—all possible candidates for blame. In fact, willpower is rarely the sole solution to any problem. Personal motivation is the "big dumb one" in your personal-change arsenal. It hunkers down, toughs it out, and pushes hard against all odds, even when the easier solution might be simply to work smarter. In this chapter you'll move away from sheer willpower and toward smarter tactics for improving your know-how. You'll learn to develop an intentional strategy to master the skills to overcome your weakness.

THE IMPORTANCE OF SKILL IN PERSONAL CHANGE

Every time you try your best to do what you know is right and you fail, there's a good chance that your failure can be traced in part to a gap in knowledge or a missing skill. Knowledge and skill can be just as important as will in any personal change program.

For example, the calories in a daily can of sweetened soft drink are enough to add fifteen pounds to your weight a year. This information isn't exactly secret, nor is it difficult to calculate, but research reveals that obese children and their parents are especially unlikely to be aware of it.[1] They have a knowledge gap.

Unpaid credit cards double their debt every four years. Again, this is common knowledge in some circles but a blind spot to most couples seeking bankruptcy counseling.[2] Smokers who rush their asthmatic children to emergency rooms are the least likely to realize that it was secondhand smoke from their cigarettes that caused the asthma attack.[3]

Our own research into problems at work revealed that 70 percent of employees who were aware that their boss was unhappy with their performance couldn't tell you what they were doing wrong or how they were going to change it.[4]

The findings are clear. Many of our personal problems are partially rooted in our *inability* to do what's required, and rarely do we think about this, because our lack of skill or knowledge sits in our blind spot. When this is the case, simply enhancing your personal ability can make a huge difference. When you learn how to *do what you can't* (by either adding a behavioral skill or becoming aware of what's happening to you), change comes faster and easier.

For instance, Changer A.J.W., who was trying to quit smoking, also realized that for the health goals she had set, she needed to lose weight too. In reviewing her crucial moments, she learned she needed to get better at recognizing her own emotions. For most of her adult life, A.J. had labeled any bad emotion "hunger" and grabbed a bag of chips and lit up a cigarette.

As A.J. developed a wider emotional vocabulary, she found other ways of identifying and responding to her feelings. Eventually A.J. learned to distinguish hunger from boredom, hunger from hurt, and hunger from worry. Then, instead of responding with a trip to the refrigerator every time she felt any emotion, she chose other, more appropriate responses to her feelings.

For instance, when bored, A.J. now sought out a stimulating conversation or an intriguing book rather than a snack. When worried, she learned to seek comfort by focusing on corrective action, not by consuming comfort food. As A.J. learned to respond to her diverse feelings in more skillful ways, it became far easier for her to avoid both smoking and snacking. By turning to Source 2 and adding the right skill, A.J. no longer required massive doses of willpower to create the change she was seeking.

TACTIC 1: START WITH A SKILL SCAN

How about you? When it comes to fighting your demons, what skills or knowledge do you lack? The answer to this may be harder than you think. Consider Changer Michael V. He became quite skilled as he perfected a life of crime and drug addiction. As a talented addict he could find drugs within minutes of entering a new city. With time and practice he became a master burglar and world-class mooch. At one point he even became an expert at Dumpster diving. And although none of these talents made it onto Michael's résumé, they were a big part of his skill repertoire.

Unfortunately, as Michael tried to transform from addicted criminal to ordinary citizen, he discovered he was missing other skills, that is, the skills for living a law-abiding and sober life. He was completely ignorant about self-control, emotional regulation (his anger often led to binge drinking), and resisting temptation, to name a few.

Or how about Sarah D., the Changer who finally broke her credit card addiction? She was a genius at kiting credit cards, hiding expenditures from her husband, and creating plausible stories, but when it came to just saying no to her shopaholic friends—well, that was a moon shot for Sarah.

Until Sarah learned how to create a livable and smart budget and then monitor her expenditures against it, her ability to invent clever stories that explained her behavior trumped her ability to spend wisely. Until

Sarah crafted a script and practiced it—a script for telling her friend that she wouldn't be shopping today (and doing it in a way that didn't look self-righteous or feel insulting)—Sarah gave in to every single request to "hit the mall."

Sarah never imagined that bringing her spending under control would require an assertiveness workshop—but it did. After studying her crucial moments (one of which was saying no to her best friend), she realized that until she mastered the ability to stand firm against an unrelenting onslaught of "Puh-leeze go with me!" from someone she really enjoyed being with, she was destined to sink deeper into debt. While Sarah had a PhD in sniffing out a bargain, she had an elementary education in responding to peer pressure. In order to move ahead with her change plan, she needed to rectify this skill imbalance.

You'll need to do the same. When it comes to your personal change project, conduct a *skill scan*—that is, scan your ability to do what's required before you implement your plan. Find out what you know and don't know as well as what you can and can't do. This can be surprisingly difficult to uncover at first, so seek help from others who are a bit further down the change path. Visit ChangeAnything .com, where you'll encounter people who are succeeding at solving problems just like yours. Find out what skills they needed to learn, and see if you'll need to do the same. You can also find new tactics, articles, books, seminars, and services that will help you as you continue your quest to do what you can't.

TACTIC 2: EMPLOY DELIBERATE PRACTICE

When it comes to learning how to do what you can't, few subjects are more resistant to learning a new behavior than people with debilitating fears—say, snake phobics. Imagine that the very sight of a snake paralyzes you. The mere uttering of the word "slither" gives you the heebie-jeebies.

Now, in order to rid yourself once and for all of the crippling fear, do you think you'd sign up for a class that teaches snake wrangling? And for the course final, do you think you'd sit by yourself in a chair and willingly drape a boa constrictor across your shoulders? Probably not.

This was the challenge renowned psychologist Albert Bandura decided to confront back in the mid-1960s when it was common therapeutic practice to put snake phobics on a couch and guide them through Freudian analysis of critical childhood events to determine the root cause of their paralyzing fear of snakes.

In truth, Bandura was disgusted that his colleagues relied on talking cures: "So, did your mother fear snakes?" He suspected that there was a shorter path. Rather than conjure primal memories, Dr. Bandura would *train* patients to handle snakes. In short, he'd teach them to do what they couldn't.

To do so, Bandura took people who had undergone decades of useless talk therapy into a lab. There he guided subjects step-by-step through a process of seeing, approaching, and eventually lifting a large serpent from a terrarium and wrapping it around their unprotected body. If they couldn't sit by themselves in a room and wrap a serpent around their shoulders, they couldn't graduate.

To effect their extraordinary transformation (remember, these were people who were so frightened by snakes that they willingly showed up at the basement of Stanford's psychology building in order to receive help), Bandura broke the challenge into small, doable parts (touching the door of the room containing a snake in a terrarium; walking arm in arm with a guide into the room—then exiting slowly; donning protective clothing and approaching the terrarium; etc.). The participants practiced each in short intervals—while receiving feedback from a coach. By following these tenets of rapid skill acquisition (formally called *deliberate practice*), 100 percent of the subjects eventually hoisted the serpent onto their shoulders and graduated.

And now for the surprising part. The entire process took about two hours![5]

So, take your pick. Option 1: you can endlessly discuss your personal challenges with friends, co-workers, and loved ones, or option 2: you can embrace a promising new skill-development tool known as deliberate practice.[6] It may be your quickest route to skilling up to any challenge. It certainly was for Patricia S.

Patricia, a high-energy critical-care nurse and nurse educator, faced a common challenge. She desperately wanted to improve her marriage. Patricia's *skill scan* helped her realize that she approached sensitive conversations with her husband, Jonathan, with the speed and subtlety of a gunslinger. As an interaction unfolded, Jonathan often struggled for words, moving his end of the conversation at a snail's pace. By the time Jonathan had figured out how to express himself, Patricia was loaded with three angry counterarguments.

Patricia recognized that if she wanted to improve her marriage, she'd have to develop the skill of conversing at *his* pace, not hers. She'd need to learn patience. She'd also need to truly listen and ask questions rather than simply judge and attack—skills she had honed mercilessly in her loud, combative upbringing.

So, she and Jonathan practiced together. They started by working on Patricia's skill of listening to her colleagues at work—also a problem Patricia faced. She and Jonathan broke the skill of listening into discrete elements, then picked a topic she needed to discuss with a colleague at work—something that was really bugging her—and then for ten or fifteen minutes (no longer) Patricia practiced while Jonathan gave her detailed feedback.

For instance, Patricia practiced taking a full breath and letting it out as she thought carefully about what the other person had just said. She practiced asking questions, and Jonathan gave her feedback when she appeared too eager to respond or too caustic in her reply. Then she tried again.

Patricia says that by following the tenets of deliberate practice she did more to improve her communication skills than she could have by reading a score of books. Of course, not only did she make progress in how she listened at work; she also learned how to apply the same skills when talking with her husband—her reason for practicing the skills in the first place.

When it comes to learning how to *do what you can't*, here's how to make the best use of deliberate practice.

Practice—and Practice for Crucial Moments. Most people think about, talk about, and think some more about what they need to do—but they never get around to actually practicing with a coach or friend. That's a mistake. Everyone needs to practice. You're no exception. And when it comes to practice, remember the oft-quoted words of legendary

NFL coach Vince Lombardi: Practice doesn't make perfect; perfect practice makes perfect.

How do you perform this "perfect" practice? Crucial moments point the way. Patricia recognized that the moments that either hurt or strengthened her marriage the most were those when she needed to discuss a problem with Jonathan. So those were the moments she prepared for and the skills she practiced. Look to your own crucial moments and ask: What do I have to be able to do to best survive those high-stakes circumstances?

Break the Skills into Small Pieces, and Practice Each Skill in Short Intervals. Patricia avoided the mistake of holding a long conversation and then seeking minor feedback at the end—when any mistakes she'd made in the conversation were already becoming part of her style. To keep the practice elements short, Patricia studied each skill, broke it into small pieces, and then practiced each piece. First she practiced managing her emotions—even when she felt she was under attack. This involved rethinking her judgments about the other person and controlling her breathing. Then she practiced the skill of restating the other person's view. Next she worked on sharing her view by using tactful and tentative language. Breaking the task into pieces made it manageable and much easier to learn.

Get Immediate Feedback against a Clear Standard, and Evaluate Your Progress. As Patricia immersed herself in deliberate practice, she quickly learned that she was on the "wrong side of her eyeballs." That is, she had an image of herself as she talked, but she couldn't see what others were seeing. So Jonathan gave her feedback—from his side of her eyeballs. He pointed out her strong tone, averting glance, and inflammatory language. Until Jonathan pointed it out, she hadn't realized that she emphasized her arguments by pointing her finger at others—as if flinging an accusation.

Prepare for Setbacks. Finally, Jonathan helped Patricia prepare for very specific crucial conversations in advance so she could be on guard for difficult twists and turns. She would also debrief conversations that didn't go well and use them as opportunities to develop greater skill in the future.

A BUSINESS EXAMPLE

Deliberate practice is complicated enough that another example might be useful here. In this case, we'll look at how Micah N. used deliberate practice to improve his ability to write project reports. He wrote several of these each week and found them tedious and time-consuming. Yet he knew his mediocre quality and efficiency at this crucial element of his job was keeping him stuck at his current pay level. So he set a goal to be able to complete a report within one hour without sacrificing any quality.

Micah began by *breaking the skills into small pieces and practicing each skill in short intervals*. These pieces were the project's purpose, its progress, immediate risks to its timeline or budget, and decisions he needed to secure from his manager. Micah began with the "Purpose" section for a single project, writing and editing it down to its bare essentials.

Next, Micah created a way to *get immediate feedback against a clear standard and evaluate his progress*. He took his model for the "Purpose" section and applied it to several other projects. He sat with a timer to see how quickly he could go from blank page to completed section. Then he compared the section to his model. After a couple of hours of this deliberate practice, Micah could consistently finish a clear and concise "Purpose" section in five minutes flat. Then he moved on to complete the same kind of practice with the other sections of his reports.

Micah also *prepared for setbacks*. Some of his reports were unique, and these remained more time-consuming. But Micah found that his practice helped even with these more customized reports. He had discovered shortcuts in writing and expression.

You too can enjoy the same success. Research shows that if you use the same tenets of deliberate practice, you can learn two or three times faster than you could if you followed less structured methods.[7]

TACTIC 3: LEARN THE WILL SKILL

Many of the toughest challenges you face are difficult because they test your willpower. Everyone knows this. But what far too few people know is that *will is a skill*, not a character trait. Willpower can be learned and strengthened like anything else, and (no surprise here) it is best learned through deliberate practice.

Consider Martha A., one of our Changers. Martha is trying to lose weight by avoiding high-calorie foods. She has a plan that includes the foods she'll eat and the foods she'll avoid. She has also identified a number of crucial moments when she is especially likely to fail. Martha's goal is to improve her willpower during these crucial moments.

For example, Martha feels at risk every time she enters an espresso shop. She can't seem to avoid ordering drinks with calorie-packed add-ons. What might be a double espresso or black coffee with five calories becomes a sixteen-ounce chocolate mocha with over five hundred calories. So her rule has been: Don't go inside espresso shops, period.

But this rule isn't ideal. Martha likes coffee drinks, and she often gets together with friends at the espresso shop near her work. She'd like to develop the willpower to walk into the shop, order a double espresso, "No cream, no sugar, please," and enjoy the company of her friends. But Martha knows she doesn't have that much willpower.

So, should Martha run the risk of going into a coffee shop to be with friends yet face a temptation she can't withstand? Or should she avoid the temptation altogether and give up on the chats with friends?

If Martha is merely going to enter the shop with her friends and stare at the high-calorie offerings, she's better off staying outside. Without some kind of plan to shore up her willpower, she'll be torturing herself needlessly.

So Martha lays out a plan, including the following list of crucial moments, ranging from least to most risky:

- Morning break. I feel like a coffee, but I don't want anything sweet. Least tempting: I can usually avoid drinking calories.
- After lunch, my co-workers and I drop by the espresso shop before returning to work. A bit more tempting: I often order a calorie-filled drink.
- Saturday morning. I haven't had breakfast. I meet friends at the espresso shop before shopping. Very tempting: I can't resist drinking five-hundred-plus calories.

- My spouse takes me to the espresso shop as a Sunday afternoon date. He orders a sweet drink and gets me one too. Extremely tempting: I can't imagine having enough willpower.

Next, Martha prepares for her crucial moments by turning to a helpful source of influence: First, she asks her husband and a co-worker to act as her coaches—to encourage her to make low-calorie choices. Just knowing the coaches are there helps her resist the temptation.

Then Martha begins deliberate practice by placing herself in a tempting situation. Her goal is to experience the desire but not give in to it. To avoid caving in, Martha brings in the main tool for enhancing her will skill. She tries several different ways of *distracting* herself. Instead of riveting her view on the caloric concoctions and dreaming of how they might taste (her usual tactic), Martha averts her eyes. Next, she steps back and reads a poster on the wall. Then she starts a conversation with a friend. As Martha continues to wait, she pulls out her cell phone and checks her e-mail. She also shifts her emotions by slowly reciting her Personal Motivation Statement in her mind and thinking about each word.

Martha learns that as she distracts herself, she dramatically reduces her cravings. She also learns that urges, even powerful ones, usually subside over fifteen to twenty minutes.[8] Martha doesn't have to distract herself endlessly. Distractions simply cause delay, and delay lessens the craving.

Next, Martha practiced her distract-and-delay tactics with increasingly difficult situations—first on an empty stomach, and then with someone encouraging her to indulge her chocolate

fantasy. Naturally, here's where it can get risky, so Martha increases
the risk only when she has a coach standing by. Her goal should be
to put herself in *reasonably* tempting situations and to develop the
skill to survive them.

It's important to be careful on this point, because there may be
situations that are impossible to withstand. For instance, many experts
suggest that alcoholics may never be able to develop enough willpower to
be safe in tempting situations. Consequently, many never walk into a bar.
Others never stock alcohol in their home. Martha decides that walking
into a coffee shop when hungry and with a friend who always encourages
her to indulge is pushing her limits, so she avoids such temptations. She
weighed the odds of caving in against the benefits of facing new temptations head-on and chose carefully. You'll have to do the same.

Fortunately, the experts do agree on one thing. The key to safe,
deliberate practice in risky situations is to have a coach nearby.[9] As you're
building will by learning how to delay and distract yourself, involve a
trusted friend who is empowered to pull you out of the situation if the
temptation turns out to be too much.

SUMMARY: DO WHAT YOU CAN'T

If you're like most people, when creating a personal change plan
you're far more likely to rely on willpower than to enhance your
skills. You figure that toughing it out is the one best response to all
of your urges. Besides, what skills could possibly help you face your
temptations?

However, as you watch effective Changers in action, you note that in
some form they learn to recognize their crucial moments, create vital

behaviors, conduct a personal skill scan, discover where they have to learn new skills, and then work on them.

Patricia responded by learning how to hold high-stakes conversations. Micah practiced the skill of creating project reports under the pressure of a deadline. Martha learned how to improve her willpower. You need to be equally vigilant when enhancing your skill set.

Start with a Skill Scan. Visit ChangeAnything.com and study the skills other people facing similar problems have had to learn (some will come as a surprise). If all you think you have to do is to stop doing the wrong thing and start doing the right thing, you haven't looked closely enough. What will it take to stop doing the wrong thing? What will it take to start doing the right thing?

Employ Deliberate Practice. What actions will you need to take? Do you know exactly what to do and say? Is the skill complicated, and if so, what are the component parts? Against what standard will you measure yourself? Who is qualified to give you feedback?

Learn the Will Skill. What is your most tempting scenario? How can you avoid the circumstance altogether? If you don't want to duck out completely, how will you withstand the temptation? Exactly how will you distract yourself? Who will help you through your toughest moments?

Sources 3 and 4
Turn Accomplices into Friends

	MOTIVATION	ABILITY
PERSONAL	1	2
SOCIAL	**3**	**4**
STRUCTURAL	5	6

You don't have to be a social scientist to know that the people around you influence you for both good and ill. You hardly have to scratch the surface of the field of social psychology to uncover a host of studies in which people fall prey to the power of social influence. For instance, in the early 1950s Solomon Asch was able to manipulate research subjects into giving a wrong answer by having a half dozen "peers" first give the same wrong answer. When they fell under the gaze of other people, two out of three research subjects gave embarrassingly incorrect answers rather than deviate from the norm.[1]

Moreover, if the people wielding social pressure are not merely peers, but individuals in a position of authority, there's almost no limit to what they can get innocent research subjects to do. It's hard to forget Stanley Milgram's haunting study wherein researchers in lab jackets were able to influence everyday citizens to administer what they thought might be lethal shocks to individuals whose only mistake had been to give a wrong answer. When the maximum social influence was applied, 90 percent of anxious subjects shocked their cohorts into silence.[2]

In a less-well-known but equally riveting study, to measure the power of hypnotism, scholars at the University of Sydney put subjects into a deep hypnotic state and then asked them to grab a highly venomous snake. Next they asked them to thrust their hand in a vat of acid, and eventually (you won't believe this), they requested that subjects throw acid into the face of one of the research assistants. Every element of the test was contrived, of course (the "venomous" snake was behind a hidden panel of glass; the "acid" was surreptitiously swapped out for colored water), but it all looked very real—*and every single one of the subjects complied*. It was an impressive demonstration of the power of hypnosis. Or so they thought.

To provide proper scientific rigor, the researchers needed a control group. They'd have to put a similar group through the same tests *without* first hypnotizing them. That way they'd be certain the hypnosis was the cause of the hypnotized subjects' absolute compliance. As they performed their control trials, the scholars watched in stunned silence as the control group behaved in *exactly the same way* as the hypnotized subjects. Every single one of the unhypnotized subjects grabbed the snake, thrust his or her hand in "acid," and threw "acid" into the assistant's face as ordered.[3]

To see if we could still demonstrate the powerful effects of social pressure (after all, most of the original research was conducted a half century ago), our team at Change Anything Labs conducted its own study. It was an attempt to get social influence working for something a bit more noble than torturing strangers or risking life and limb. We hoped to harness it in the service of getting kids to wash their hands.

We asked kids to put together a puzzle. At the end of each round, and as a reward for putting the puzzle together correctly, the subjects were given tantalizing cupcakes, but they first needed to wash their hands with the antiseptic gel nearby because—as we told them—"a boy from a previous group had touched the puzzle and, well, he had the sniffles."

Left to their own desires, every single one of the kids rushed to the cupcakes, not pausing to wash. What would it take to get them to gel up? Highlighting the germs wasn't enough. So we tried moving the gel closer to the action. No takers. Having the kids practice washing prior to assembling the puzzle also yielded no change. But in the round where one of the kids paused as her peers rushed to the cupcakes and reminded them, "Don't forget to wash your hands!" eleven out of twelve subjects complied. (To see this experiment in action, go to ChangeAnything.com/exclusive.) After decades of studies, people are still people. We're still social animals.

That means if you're spending too much, you're probably not alone. If you're hooked on video games, well, that too is often a social event. If your body's in slow decline as you transform into a dreaded couch potato, even if you watch TV alone there are literally thousands of people out there doing their level best to keep you nestled in a couch and watching their advertisements.

We're interested in helping you break free of blindness about the role others currently play in the habit you're trying to change. More importantly, we're going to help you find ways to engage their practically irresistible influence in the service of your goals. The goal is *not* for you to simply stand against the overwhelming sway of peer pressure—but to make it work *for* you.

TACTIC 1: KNOW WHO'S A FRIEND
AND WHO'S AN ACCOMPLICE

When it comes to your bad habits, you have two kinds of people around you: friends and accomplices. Friends help keep you on the road to health, happiness, and success. Accomplices do the opposite. Accomplices aid and abet the "crime" of your current bad habit.

You may inaccurately call some of your accomplices "friends" because you enjoy being with them. However, if they either enable or encourage you to behave in unwise ways—lower your aspirations, take a drink, buy a gadget, skip a workout session—they're acting as accomplices.

This may sound harsh—but let's be clear: The people around you don't have to have an agenda to be accomplices. What makes them accomplices is not having bad intentions, but exerting bad influence.

So, if you hope to change tough habits in your life, one of the most important steps you'll need to take is to distinguish between those around you who are acting as friends and those who are acting as accomplices.

ACCOMPLICES

The Obvious. As you look around for people who are enticing and enabling your unhealthy behavior, you'll find that some are easy to spot. Your most obvious accomplices are those who stand to make money if you fail or lose an excuse for their own bad habits if you succeed. The attractive server in the restaurant who gushes about the delicious desserts wants your money, not your health. The pals who equate your newfound ambition at work as selling out to the Man want your collusion, not your success.

The Not So Obvious. Then there are others out there whom you may not care about or even notice. Nevertheless, their very existence has a strong influence on your choices. Believe it or not, many of your accomplices do nothing more than cast a shadow that affects your choices. Here's how it works.

Michael E., one of our intrepid Changers, suffered from an eating problem that quietly escalated without his realizing it—due to the quiet, unnoticed accomplices surrounding him. In his own words, he "missed the moment he crossed the line from being *big* to being *obese*." Michael didn't recognize how obese he was becoming until one day when he saw a picture of a seriously overweight fellow on a bulletin board at work. The longer he stared at the photo, the more eerie he felt. It took a minute before Michael realized that *he* was the guy in the picture.

Models—Who's Normal?

How could Michael have missed what had happened to him? He had a mirror. He had scales. But he also lived in a world made up of friends, co-workers, and strangers who had gradually gained weight right along with him. These unwitting accomplices helped him change his view of what was average, acceptable, and reasonable—and he didn't even know it.

Nicholas Christakis, a Harvard sociologist, has carefully studied this subtle phenomenon. After combing through thirty years of data gathered from twelve thousand residents of Framingham, Massachusetts, Christakis discovered that obesity is at least partly *infectious*. People appear to catch it from each other. He found that having obese friends increases your chance of following suit by a whopping 57 percent.[4]

How does this frightening phenomenon work? The best explanation is that the people we see around us determine our view of what's normal. Then (as was the case with Michael) when we gain weight, we know we're gaining weight, but we don't see ourselves as obese. Why? Because we're like everyone else around us, and that makes us normal, and normal people are normal, not obese.

Unfortunately, the people around us affect us in more profound ways than simply giving us camouflage. If, for example, your colleagues at work are resentful of management, deride those with ambition, and elevate politics over professionalism, this "norm" communicates what's acceptable. Since everyone is doing it, who would have the gall to ridicule you for doing the same? Surely your friends, co-workers, and loved ones will still accept you because they're modeling the same "normal" thing you're doing.

Sadly, one of the most active things our colleagues do to change our sense of what is acceptable is to remain silent. These hard-to-see co-conspirators would like to help us remain on the right path, but they don't quite know how to lend a hand.

For example, while doing research for what eventually became known as the Silence Kills study,[5] we at the Change Anything Labs learned of a rather gruff and commanding anesthesiologist who had undiagnosed Alzheimer's. Nurses and physicians failed to speak up to him, thinking that when he failed to follow protocol maybe he was just distracted—plus they didn't want to offend him or appear accusatory.

Finally, the fellow lost track of what he was doing during a child's surgery. A nurse ran to get another anesthesiologist to fill in—and the truth came out. Someone almost had to die before people were willing to speak up.

When it comes to silently watching others act in unhealthy ways, we've all done it. We've all clammed up and nervously (sometimes painfully) watched our friends sink into deeper trouble. Each time we decide to say nothing, we become a silent accomplice.

Unfortunately, when it comes to our own unhealthy behavior, we may be surrounded by silent, tortured accomplices who, if they only felt comfortable, would give us a tremendous boost in the right direction.

One final way accomplices affect our behavior comes in the form of lowered aspirations. For example, when Philippa Clarke, an epidemiologist at the University of Michigan, studied forty-year-old subjects who had been overweight since adolescence, she found a link between peer pressure and several different negative outcomes.

Compared to forty-year-olds who had gradually gained weight after graduating from high school, those who had been chronically overweight since age nineteen were more likely to be less educated, unemployed or on welfare, and without a partner. How does this work? According to Clarke, the chronically overweight population probably experienced discrimination as children that lowered their self-esteem, which, in turn lowered their aspirations.[6] Like it or not, peers not only help define what is normal, but also help define what is possible.

Hosts: Who Sets the Agenda?

The next group of accomplices is quite visible and active in our lives. They don't want us to suffer, per se, but they do enjoy sharing our weaknesses, and they're more than willing to speak up. This group doesn't just passively communicate what's normal; they decide what's normal at regular get-togethers. In so doing, they act as hosts to our unhelpful choices.

For instance, consider Renee C., a Changer who had trouble controlling her spending. Before she was able to turn herself around, Renee maxed out eight credit cards and was spending $280 per month on interest alone—throwing her further into debt and closer to bankruptcy each month. How did Renee get to this point?

It turns out that Renee had a handful of wealthy female friends whose income was three or four times hers—but whom Renee did her best to match dollar for dollar by purchasing gourmet dinners, high-fashion shoes, and spa vacations. That is, she kept pace—until one day she found herself up to her neck in debt. Naturally, no one forced Renee to put on a pair of eight-hundred-dollar Jimmy Choo sandals, or eat a pricey truffle side dish, but the events that brought her and her friends together always involved commerce. Pricey commerce—coupled with a good time with "friends."

Of course, with friends like these . . . If you're ever to take control of your choices, you'll have to take control of the social events that shape those choices. If the meetings, lunches, social circles, and other rituals you attend encourage or enable the habits you're trying to stop, you'll need to recognize these influences for what they are. These associations amplify the effects of accomplices, not friends.

Scan for events and hosts that make your changes more difficult. Then either take charge of the event or take leave of it.

It gets worse. If you're finding it particularly tough to change, it's very possible that you have people around you who actively hold you accountable to a bad habit.

For instance, seventeen-year-old Rachel L. learned that her dearest "friend" cared far more about their shared vice than about their friendship. Rachel came to this realization one day when she hit rock bottom (she was taking Vicodin and several other prescription medications every day just to function) and ran to her best girlfriend, Bryn, to seek solace. Rachel poured out her heart to her lifelong buddy by sharing her desire to feel clean, take charge of her urges, and eventually go to college. Bryn remained quiet. When Rachel finally finished sharing her dream, Bryn looked at her coldly and remarked, "So now you're better than me?"

That's the response of a pretty aggressive accomplice. Maybe even a bully. In essence, Bryn was holding Rachel accountable to her bad habit.

As Rachel built a careful plan to break her prescription drug addiction, ironically she got nothing but grief from Bryn. Her former best friend ridiculed her, threatened her, tempted her, pled with her, and did everything else she could imagine to keep Rachel hooked on the drugs they had shared for years. Only by distancing herself from her former best friend was Rachel able to break free of her negative influence.

What does all of this talk of accomplices mean? If you want to turn social influence in your favor, you'll have to identify accomplices of all kinds: the subtle, the blatant, the hosts who are holding you to the old standard. Take a quick inventory. Who will speak up if you fail to follow the old, unhealthy norms? Who will blow a whistle when you begin playing by new, healthy rules? Whom do you worry about disappointing, receiving criticism from, or even incurring wrath from? These are your accomplices.

FRIENDS

Coaches and Fans: Who Yells, Helps, and Cheers?

Now let's turn our attention to our biggest change allies. These are the individuals who—actively and sometimes almost imperceptibly—help keep us on the path to success by modeling good choices, speaking up, holding us accountable, offering advice, and cheering us on.

In all likelihood you have friends who already play these roles. Some play the role of informal *coach* by reminding us of the rules, watching our performance, and teaching us how to succeed. Other friends stand on the sidelines, watch us in action, and cheer our every success. These priceless, encouraging friends play the role of *fan*.

Here's how these two types of friends can work for you.

Coaches

Virtually all of the Changers we studied benefited from the help of informal coaches. For instance, Sandy M. found her marriage taking a downward spiral. Disagreements with her partner were becoming more frequent, vitriolic, and harmful. At first Sandy blamed her partner for all of their problems, but as she began to examine her own behavior, she realized that she was acting in unhelpful ways as well. Standing nearby and feeding her unhelpful behaviors were several vocal accomplices.

Sandy had fallen into the habit of comparing "dumb husband" stories with anyone who would affirm her view that he was the cause of the trouble in their marriage. She and a work colleague exchanged "dumb husband" jokes. With her sister-in-law she shared "loser husband" stories. Of course, her gossiping with accomplices solved no problems, while causing her to feel increasingly upset, justified, and smug.

So Sandy finally traded her accomplices in for a skilled coach. She distanced herself from those who were cynical about their marriages and connected with a counselor who helped her see not just the negative but also some of the positive elements of her relationship. Eventually both Sandy and her husband teamed up with the counselor, who coached them toward better ways of relating to each other. Both stopped talking about each other behind his or her back. Both benefited from replacing accomplices with a positive coach.

Virtually all of our Changers used coaches in similar ways. Addicts joined groups filled with specialists who teach new life skills. Spenders took courses from experts in both finances and behavioral change. Executives often gained the help of personal coaches who taught them interpersonal skills. Of course, millions of people use coaches to learn how to exercise and eat in more healthy ways.

So as you lay out your own change plan, find coaches.

Fans

Friends can help in another way. In addition to positively *enabling* you as a coach, friends can turn into fans by providing the motivation you need to make it through the dog days of personal change. Like any loyal fan, they can stand on the sidelines and cheer your success or gently chide your failures.

For example, Michael E., the fellow we met earlier who was trying to overcome obesity, loves the feeling of the real-time accountability he experiences from the website he uses to track his daily exercise. The site allows him to connect with others who will check up on his progress. Every morning at the crack of dawn he knows there are two other guys in other areas of the world who are limbering up to start their own exercise routines. When Michael logs in to the website and reports for duty, they let him know they're watching him.

Michael explains, "Just the feeling that I know they'll be waiting for me gives me a little extra push to be there every day." His buddies are taking attendance, and he feels accountable to be there for roll call. In that sense they are peer coaches. But beyond accountability, he enjoys the camaraderie and sense of accomplishment he gets when they applaud his success. They are likewise his daily fans.

More and more people are learning how to turn colleagues into fans. For example, note how the Care Product Institute (CPI) uses fans to help diabetics better manage their blood-sugar levels.

It's hard to criticize diabetics who fail to stay with their health regime when you realize that one of their vital behaviors involves jabbing their fingertip with a sharp pin six times a day every single day. Research shows that fewer than a third of diabetics perform this test as often as they should—even with full knowledge that their dereliction is likely to lead to amputations, blindness, or death.[7]

Now, if threats of this magnitude don't change most diabetics' behavior, what will?

CPI discovered that you can substantially increase people's compliance by simply ratting them out to their friends.[8] To take advantage of this powerful source of influence, designers at CPI created a device that e-mails information about the patient's blood sugar—not to the doctor, but to friends and family. Then, as you might suspect, the friends and family members immediately contact the reluctant finger prickers and encourage them to get back on the regime. After just a little positive (or negative) reaction from friends and family, many diabetics begin testing as they should.

Fans. We need more of these lovely people around us.

REDO THE MATH

Now that you've identified the people around you who typically aid and abet the habits you want to change, it's time to get the math working in your favor. In the end, you'll want your world to be made up of more friends and fewer accomplices. In an ideal world, you'll want all friends and no accomplices.

The good news is that you won't have to find all new friends, loved ones, and co-workers. Most of your acquaintances will simply have to change how they treat you. And most will be glad to do so.

TACTIC 2: REDEFINE "NORMAL"

To help blunt the power of accomplices and unhealthy role models, take note of how they're affecting your vision of what's normal. Don't be fooled by people who bandy around the words "everybody" and "normal" as a means of justifying their own unhealthy behavior. Instead, call it unhealthy, unwise, or even dangerous—but never call it normal.

For instance, consider the following interaction, which was recently broadcast on National Public Radio. An expert was discussing the pros and cons of multitasking when an excited listener called in to explain that his life was so horribly busy that he needed to multitask just to keep up. In his case, driving to and from work provided him with a wonderful opportunity to send text messages to friends and associates—who routinely sent text messages back (also while driving). In short, "every-one" was texting while driving, and this was a big help in his life.

After an awkward pause, the expert responded, "You can call what you're doing multitasking if you like; I call it being enormously unsafe. When you text and drive, you're far more likely to get in an accident."[9] By intervening in this way, the expert prodded the audience's perception of what's normal for drivers.

You have to do the same—for yourself. If you continue to measure yourself against norms set by disinterested accomplices, you may be on a path to ruin. Consider the words of an executive friend of ours who took undeserved solace in studying his competitors.

"At first," the executive explained, "we were worried by the downturn in the economy. But when we learned we were doing about as well as our chief competitor, we stopped fretting. Then one day our competitor went bankrupt, and it wasn't long until we followed suit. I can't believe how stupid we were. It was as if we were measuring ourselves against a corpse—and feeling pretty healthy by comparison."

Perhaps the best response to a shifting sense of normalcy is to quit making external comparisons in the first place. Rise above the shared sense of what is common or acceptable. To do so, ask yourself two questions. How do you want to live and feel? And who do you want to be?

TACTIC 3: HOLD A TRANSFORMATION CONVERSATION

As numerous as your accomplices may be, there is good news in the fact that you can transform many into coaches and fans by using one simple method. Hold a *transformation conversation*. Don't wait for people to read your mind. Tell them exactly what you want and need.

For example, give your mute accomplices who are dying to help you out permission to speak up. Let your well-intended friends know what they need to do to help rather than hurt you. And put those who try to coach you back into old habits on notice. As far as your future relationship is concerned, you're going to do what's right for you, period.

Start the transformation conversation by asking others for their help. Don't blame others, but do explain the role they're unintentionally playing in your unhealthy behavior. By focusing on their *effect* rather than blaming them for bad *intent*, you decrease the chance they'll feel defensive. Then ask for a new and healthier relationship—you want them to be friends. Finally, explain exactly what you want them to do. For example: "If you hear me ordering high-calorie food at the restaurant, feel free to encourage me to choose a more healthy selection."

Now for the best news. Every time you transform an accomplice into a friend, you win twice. You remove the influence of someone who is pulling against you while adding someone who is pulling for you. Transforming an accomplice into a friend gives you double the influence. Because of this dual effect, this simple transaction can be your most powerful tool for social influence.

TACTIC 4: ADD NEW FRIENDS

The easiest way to exploit the power of social influence is to add new friends. Find those people who either share your goal or are interested in offering you support. Engage them as coaches or fans. Or just hang out with them to help you see a new "normal." Most will be glad to help. Few things kick-start a relationship faster than a sincere request for assistance from a person with a worthwhile purpose.

Changer Ron M. decided it was time for a change when his sales manager put him on probation. His sales had been anemic for months, and he knew his habits would have to change if he was to keep his job. He started by altering his lunch habits. Ron realized that he typically socialized with the more cynical, lower-performing members of his sales team and concluded that if he was to improve his results, he needed the influence of those with a different perspective. At first it felt awkward, as he felt abnormal around some of his more successful colleagues. But he began to relish that feeling of discomfort as his attitudes and goals began to align with this new "normal." Within a quarter he was off probation and progressing rapidly.

If you'd like to add several new friends at once, join associations and social networks made up of people who are working on the same problem you're trying to conquer. For instance, Michael E. started his incredibly successful weight-loss plan by publicly announcing his intentions on Facebook.

"I immediately got a message back from a guy at my church," Michael explains. "We were friends, but I didn't know he was involved in the same program. We became close friends and bounced things off one another and encouraged each other all the time."

TACTIC 5: DISTANCE YOURSELF FROM THE UNWILLING

Not everyone you associate with will be willing to transform from accomplice to friend. In some instances you'll have to distance yourself from individuals who repeatedly encourage or enable your bad habits. More often than not, this distancing evolves naturally and painlessly. For example, people who increase their exercise find more common interests with others who exercise. Soon they're spending more time together. Those who want to eat more healthily start lunching with a different mix of people, who have similar dietary interests.

But you can't forget the desperate accomplices who will fight to keep you entrenched in your old ways. When Michael V. returned home from prison and decided to abandon his life of crime, alcohol, and drugs, he had to cut off contact with many of his old pals. He started by adding new friends. He joined AA, where he found several people who served as both coaches and fans. He also met with old acquaintances and held a transformation conversation. Most were willing to become fans and coaches.

But when it came to Michael's best friend, Kirby—the guy who had been best man at his wedding—he found that Kirby didn't want to be a friend. He wanted to be a drinking buddy. Eventually Michael decided that he was tired of fighting Kirby's constant invitations and ridicule, so "in one of the toughest conversations I ever had," he ended the relationship. As you might imagine, distancing yourself from accomplices who were once good buddies (or maybe even loved ones) involves complicated value trade-offs and can be quite painful. We offer no advice other than that you not underestimate the role fans, coaches, and accomplices play in your life.

WHAT CAN YOU EXPECT?

If you stop right now and list the friends and accomplices who currently make up your world, and if you then start shifting the math in your favor by transforming and eliminating accomplices—while simultaneously making new friends—you'll dramatically increase your chances for success.

How dramatically? Our research findings have been encouraging. In a recent study conducted at the Change Anything Labs, we asked thirty-four hundred people to talk about their success and failure at changing everything from addictions to fitness, and the findings were remarkable.

The data revealed that accomplices frequently drag people back into their habits—no surprise there. But the friends had nothing short of an astounding impact. People with a half dozen active friends (who are playing the role of coach or fan) *are almost 40 percent more likely to succeed* than those with fewer than a half dozen friends![10]

So, it's time for you to transform your world from a mishmash of accomplices (models and hosts) and friends (coaches and fans) who are organized around your old habits into a team of highly functioning friends. When you see clearly the difference between a friend and an accomplice, and take action to transform accomplices into friends, you're no longer blind and outnumbered. Get the crowd behind you, and you can change anything.

SUMMARY: TURN ACCOMPLICES INTO FRIENDS

Know Who's a Friend and Who's an Accomplice. Be aware of the people who influence your life, and determine whether they are friends (helping you meet your goals) or accomplices (who distract you from or blatantly undermine your change efforts). Accomplices can hold us back often by just establishing a view of "normal" that keeps us in our bad habits. Friends are those who coach us through enacting our change or who cheer our victories. Ultimately, you want more friends and fewer accomplices. You can go to ChangeAnything.com/exclusive and use our Friends and Accomplices Inventory to help you see what's happening today and get tips for turning accomplices into friends.

Redefine "Normal." Take a look at how accomplices may be affecting your view of what's normal. If you continue to measure yourself against unhealthy or unrealistic "norms," your change plan is at risk. Ask yourself two questions: How do you want to live and feel? And who do you want to be?

Hold a Transformation Conversation. You can help transform acquaintances, loved ones, and co-workers into helpful friends by holding a *transformation conversation*. Start by asking others for their help. Explain the role they're playing in making change harder or less pleasant for you, and then share how you'd like them to help you succeed.

Add New Friends. Find people who are interested in supporting your change effort or new behaviors. Spend time with them to get coaching or to help you pick up a new "normal." This can include joining an existing group or social network, or just changing some of your associations.

Distance Yourself from the Unwilling. Just as you need to surround yourself with friends, you need to separate yourself from accomplices who can't or won't support your efforts. Often this occurs naturally as you make other life changes. But occasionally you will have to deliberately separate yourself from those who do their best to keep you from changing.

Source 5

Invert the Economy

	MOTIVATION	ABILITY
PERSONAL	1	2
SOCIAL	3	4
STRUCTURAL	5	6

THE INSIDIOUS IMPACT OF INCENTIVES

We'll start this chapter by examining a mistake committed by a rather large consulting firm. Since this particular firm made money only when the consultants were working in the field and billing for their time, the senior partners came up with a plan to keep them on the road: "The Road Warrior of the Year." This title was awarded to the consultant who logged the most billable days. To give the award real kick, the partners threw in a substantial cash prize.

For four consecutive years, "Road Warriors" gladly accepted the prize, took the generous cash reward, and then quit the firm—citing (you guessed it) work-life balance issues. It seems the winners were away from home too often.

So, what went wrong here? The incentive system, of course. The partners had long learned that if they wanted to motivate their consultants to act in new and different ways, they had to link the targeted behavior to perks, or bonuses, or hefty prizes of some kind. Cash money got and kept their attention.

But that same cash award also caused the firm unwanted turnover. In this case, the cash award motivated a behavior that couldn't be sustained. On other occasions incentives motivate a behavior that *can* be sustained, but it's the wrong behavior. This is probably the case with many of your own unhealthy habits.

For example, walk into a fast-food restaurant and a clerk cheerfully gives you a frequent-eater card. It rewards you for eating more, not less—consume eighty thousand calories and get a free meatball sandwich. The more you use certain credit cards, the bigger the cash award or travel points they give you at the end of the year. You can almost *feel* yourself getting closer to your dream vacation every time you swipe the card!

Sometimes it's the pricing itself that drives the wrong behavior. For instance, over the past thirty years the price of unhealthy food has declined while the price of fruits and vegetables has risen substantially. Guess what we're buying more of?

On other occasions it's the *timing* of the expenditure that keeps us in the dark. Consider how many of the long-term costs of our bad habits remain distant and out of mind while the pleasurable benefits show up in vivid, living color *right now*.

For example, in the U.S. obesity costs the average person an extra $1,429 per year in increased health care costs.[1] But since we're not required to set aside money for every burger we consume (to cover the real financial cost of the burger), the long-term costs of carrying extra weight remain invisible.

What if we turned this all around? What if we inverted the economy? Imagine how different our choices might be if our PayPal account were instantly charged for every unhealthy action we took or credited for our healthy behaviors—based upon the *real* economics of the situation. For example, if an insensitive comment moved us a step closer to divorce, we'd get dinged a thousand dollars. (Research shows that a breakup reduces an individual's net worth by an average of 77 percent.)[2]

Or what if each time we failed to address development needs from a performance appraisal, our next paycheck were docked 5 percent? (Eighty-five percent of the people we recently polled said they have lost out on promotions or pay increases because they didn't adequately address a boss's concerns.)[3]

Would inverting the economics in such a bizarre way help us behave in more healthy ways? Yes. For instance, recovering cocaine addicts were 23 percent more successful at adhering to a medical regime when given a small gift certificate for every week they passed a drug test.[4]

Or watch what happens to tobacco usage as excise taxes increase. Tax smoking, and it drops—along with its effects. The American Cancer Society Cancer Action Network recently announced that a federal tobacco tax increase of a dollar per pack "would prevent more than 1 million smoking-related deaths and deter nearly 2.3 million U.S. children from becoming lifelong tobacco users."[5]

What's equally fascinating is the fact that it's not just others or the government who can use incentives to change our behavior. *We're also more likely to change if we invert the economy ourselves.* We can actually bribe and threaten ourselves to change.

Here are some tactics you can use to get Source 5 working for you.

TACTIC 1: USE CARROTS AND THE THREAT OF LOSING CARROTS

Consider how incentives gave a real career boost to Rudy K., one of our Changers. When Rudy first took a job as the IT support guy at a small import company, he felt lucky. He and his high school buddies hadn't exactly been preparing themselves for the future.

Rudy explains: "While the kids who were going on to college studied physics, calculus, and the like, my friends and I preferred to travel to Azeroth, where we pretended to be Orcs while ruling the World of Warcraft. And we had no intention of changing. We'd stay away from college, live in our parents' basements, and play video games until our thumbs exploded."

This all changed rather suddenly the day Rudy landed a job in IT support, and then it took an even larger turn when Rudy's boss told Rudy that he was gifted with all things computer related and encouraged him to move from fixing e-mail problems to helping perfect the company's customer-support software. Designing software would be a better job, but in order to qualify, Rudy would have to take several college classes—both at night and on weekends—and that would cut into his game time.

However, when Rudy's boss suggested that Rudy was "a bit of a math whiz" and that he could eventually qualify for a more interesting and higher-paying job, Rudy decided to take classes—despite the fact that he'd have to trade in his Orc battle-ax for a textbook. Listen in as Rudy explains how several sources of influence (including incentives) helped him become a person he'd never imagined he could be.

"When my boss told me I had a gift for working with computers, it gave me a whole new view into myself. Maybe I could turn my gaming passion into something useful. Maybe I could even take college classes. And then when my boss found out that school intimidated me, he helped me improve my study habits. He even got permission for me to borrow a laptop that the company was no longer using. Eventually when he saw me heading off to classes each night, my boss assigned me to work for an hour a day with a top software engineer from his team, who became my mentor.

"But it still wasn't enough. The thought of studying nights and weekends was discouraging. Plus the better job seemed so far off. Then I built in an incentive. I set goals for attending class and doing homework each week, and every time I hit the goal, I would take my girlfriend to a restaurant I really liked.

"All of the help and encouragement focused attention on my long-term goal of bettering my career. But it was the date at the end of the week that helped me make it to every class, get up early to do homework, succeed in school, and eventually get the promotion."

TAKE ADVANTAGE OF "LOSS AVERSION"

This next concept draws from a Nobel Prize—winning idea. For years, Daniel Kahneman[6] and other behavioral economists have demonstrated that we humans have a bizarre quirk hardwired into us. That is, we are far more motivated to avoid loss than we are motivated to receive an equivalent gain.

The Change Anything Labs found the same thing recently when we interviewed customers salivating around an Apple store while waiting for the release of a new iPhone. On average, those who just got a phone wouldn't part with it for a dime less than $1,218 over the purchase price.

Those who were worried the phones might sell out before they got to the front of the line wouldn't pay more than an average of $97 over the purchase price to get one. In a sense, these typical customers were twelve times more motivated to avoid losing an iPhone than they were to get one. Strange, isn't it?[7]

This propensity to place a higher premium on a loss than on a gain is known as "loss aversion." The implications to personal change are quite clear. If you put something you value at risk, you might be more likely to change than if you merely rely on bonuses, prizes, and other incentives.

But how could this be? Where did this focus on the negative come from in the first place? When you think about it, loss aversion has served human beings quite well. In fact, it has actually kept us alive. Imagine an unfortunate prehistoric being who paid more attention to, say, a heavy-laden fruit tree than to an attacking saber-toothed tiger.

"Oh, look! A tree filled with lovely fruit."

"Growl. Crunch. Gulp."

No such fellow would have lived long enough to pass on his genes. But the guy who first looked for danger and then looked for pleasantries would have lived to tell about it. So that's what we modern-day humans do. We give heightened attention to any potential loss.

Change agents have been taking advantage of this human idio-syncrasy for decades. A powerful example comes from Yale behavioral economist Dean Karlan. He invited smokers in the Philippines who were trying to quit to slowly cut back the number of cigarettes they smoked each day. He also had them place the money they would have spent on the additional cigarettes into a savings account.

Six and twelve months later they were given urine tests to determine whether they had stopped smoking. Those who failed the test would have to turn their savings over to charity. Compared to a control group that did not use this self-imposed financial punishment, experimental subjects kicked the habit 50 percent more frequently. Not surprisingly, the more money the subjects put at risk, the higher their likelihood of changing.[8]

So, how can you use loss aversion to your own advantage? Put something you care about at risk. Bet on your own success. Here's how Changer Kyle N. used loss aversion to become more physically fit.

"I was having trouble exercising regularly, so I hired a fitness expert to meet with me once a week, teach me how to use the gym's equipment, and provide me with dietary assistance. The guy helped me learn the various exercises, and that made it easier, plus there's no doubt that having someone to chat with helped keep me motivated as well.

"But do you know what the real incentive was?" Kyle continues.

"I came to realize that the biggest reason I showed up week after week was because I couldn't stand the thought of paying for an expert and then not taking advantage of the resource. The idea of losing money always propelled me back into the gym. Plus my wife felt the same way. 'It's Monday!' she would exclaim. 'What do you mean you're not going to the gym? You already paid for it!'"

The power of loss aversion hasn't gone unnoticed by those who currently design personal-improvement websites. For example, the website stickK.com pioneered the practice of inviting participants to set up goals and pony up some amount of money; participants lose a portion of that money to the recipient of their choice each time they fail to meet a goal. Like others who have made use of loss aversion, stickK users have found that when they invert an existing economy, good behavior becomes a bit easier to embrace.

TACTIC 2: USE INCENTIVES IN MODERATION AND IN COMBINATION

IN MODERATION

As you watch TV programs that showcase real people who are practically tortured into losing weight—for enormous prizes—you're left wondering how well their over-the-top methods actually work. Sure, when the stakes are high enough, you can get people to put themselves through a grueling boot-camp-like regime, but what happens when the contestants return home? Once they face their old circumstances—and huge incentives are no longer in play—won't they revert to their old ways? Many do.[9]

In a similar vein, when a rather well-known movie star became a weight-loss spokesperson and was paid a lot of money for each pound she lost while using the advertised product, you had to wonder—What would happen when she hit her goal and the massive incentive was removed? Wouldn't she revert to her previous habits and weight? She did.[10]

Actually, the idea that a heavy reliance on external rewards just might backfire has long been a topic of research. In the early seventies, renowned scholar Mark Lepper conducted a pivotal study at Stanford University's famous research lab—Bing Nursery School.[11] Lepper and his team wanted to know if offering extrinsic rewards for a task that is already intrinsically pleasing might make the task itself seem less satisfying.

So Lepper rewarded nursery school children with their favorite

snack every time they played with their favorite toy. As the kids continued to receive a goody for playing with a toy that they obviously liked,
it wasn't long until they chose to play with their favorite toy less often.
Why? Lepper concluded that it was because when you give the kids
a snack for playing with something that used to be fun, they're left
wondering, How fun can the game be if I have to be rewarded every
time I play with it?

With this in mind, we'd like to add a caveat to our advice that
you ought to use incentives. Don't fall for big incentives thinking that
they're more likely to yield big results. A large incentive often becomes
an end in itself, and when it's removed, so goes your primary source
of motivation.

So, use incentives, but use them *in moderation*. It typically
takes only small rewards to work their magic. For instance, you hit
a weight-loss goal and buy a new blouse; you stick to your exercise
regimen and you reward yourself with a fly-fishing afternoon with
your son.

IN COMBINATION

Changer Rachel C. illustrates how simple rewards are best used not
only in moderation but also in combination with social and personal
motivators.

Here's Rachel's story. After years of alcohol and drug addiction, she
decided to faithfully follow a twelve-step program. At her first group
meeting Rachel's sponsor gave her a plastic poker chip and explained
that this small token was a bet on her sobriety. Her sponsor would give
her a genuine chip when she made it through the next six months sober.
With all her heart and soul Rachel wanted the real chip and all that it

meant—and after six months of hard work, she stood in front of a cheering crowd and was awarded her chip for six months of sobriety. It was a solid, heavy, brass medallion.

Later that day while sitting in her room, Rachel gazed at the medallion, turned it over in her hand, felt its weight, and wept with joy. That chip meant the world to her. Of course she didn't endure all her sufferings and effort for the six-month chip alone—she desperately intended to be sober for all the right reasons. However, earning the medallion symbolized her success in becoming the person she wanted to be (her personal motivation). Plus she proudly shared it with her friends, who celebrated her progress (her social motivation). Rachel's brass medallion was the perfect example of using incentives in moderation (it cost very little) and in combination (it worked hand in hand with—rather than overshadowed—both personal and social motivators).

TACTIC 3: REWARD SMALL WINS

For our final tactic, let's return to one of the concepts we shared earlier—large, long-term goals become far more effective when they're broken into smaller, short-term ones. This idea of using proximal goals has been around for decades but for years was never actually proven in the lab because whenever researchers gave one group of subjects a series of short-term goals and compared them to another group that received one long-term goal, subjects who were given the longer goal always broke it up into pieces in their minds, making short-term goals of their own and destroying the elegant design of the experiment.[12] They did the math in their heads and eliminated the experimental effect.

Fortunately, the research problem was eventually solved when Albert Bandura gave long-term goals to people who didn't know how to divide. That's right; he used children who were struggling with basic arithmetic. He gave them either long-term goals (finish all forty-two pages of subtraction problems by the end of the seventh session) or short-term goals (finish six pages of subtraction problems every session). The kids who were given the long-term goal couldn't divide, so they couldn't mentally break the task into shorter pieces in order to motivate themselves. Sure enough, they finished far fewer problems.[13]

The now-proven tactic of using many small goals rather than one huge goal is especially important when it's applied to incentives. Never make the mistake of attaching rewards to achieving your *ultimate* goal ("When I get that promotion, I'll buy a new car" or "I'll buy a complete new wardrobe when I drop fifty pounds"). After all, your biggest risk with any long-term change project is not that you'll fail *at the end* but that you'll drop out *at the beginning*.

As you reward yourself frequently and in small increments, also take care to reward the right thing. Reward your actions, not your results. Results are often out of your control (at least in the moment), so link your incentives to something you can control—your vital behaviors. *Reward what you do, not what you achieve.*

For example, Jose G. found that the most noxious parts of his new exercise regime weren't the jogging or swimming—those days he sort of liked—it was the weight lifting that bummed him out. So Jose built a special reward into the two days a week he pumped iron. He found a chocolate-flavored protein shake he thought was delicious (and was approved by his coach) and appointed Tuesdays and Thursdays as his "Chocolate-Shake Days."

Rather than waiting until he lost five inches off his waistline or until he could bench-press 250 pounds, Jose rewarded the vital behavior of simply completing his weight-lifting day. He looked puzzled when he explained, "I guess I could have a chocolate protein shake any day I wanted, but the fact that I *give it to myself* just for completing my weight-lifting day made me feel more in control and able to meet my goals."

SUMMARY: INVERT THE ECONOMY

As we're doing our best to improve our lives, few of us think to use incentives as a means of motivating healthy behavior. Either we forget all about them or we do recall the importance incentives play in motivating behavior—but for others, not for us. We figure we're above such a transparent and simple tool. We think to ourselves, "I don't need incentives. I can tough it out on my own!"—falling once again into the willpower trap.

This needs to change. It needs to change not only because incentives can help but also because the current "economy" is probably either subsidizing or rewarding your bad habits—or both!

As part of a six-source change plan in which you develop your own incentives, remember the following.

Use Carrots and the Threat of Losing Carrots. Be honest. Are you thinking that adding your own incentives or creating your own losses won't do you much good? If so, reconsider your stance. Bolster willpower and peer pressure with extrinsic rewards.

Use Incentives in Moderation and in Combination. What are some inexpensive but meaningful rewards you might use to your benefit? To see how other people have made an effective use of incentives, visit our website at ChangeAnything.com/exclusive.

Reward Small Wins. What are your vital behaviors? What specific actions that are under your control should you reward? How long should you go before creating a small celebration? What can you do within that time frame?

Source 6
Control Your Space

	MOTIVATION	ABILITY
PERSONAL	1	2
SOCIAL	3	4
STRUCTURAL	5	6

A couple of years ago, our team at the Change Anything Labs brought twenty tired and hungry ten-year-old soccer players together for a macaroni-and-cheese feast. We were replicating a study done by Brian Wansink and discussed in his fascinating book *Mindless Eating: Why We Eat More Than We Think*. This was no ordinary macaroni and cheese—it was a scrumptious blend of delicious cheddar, perfectly finished noodles, and savory seasonings that made the kids drool with delight.

As the kids arrived, we assigned them to two different tables—each set up in a different room. As we gave the go-ahead nod, the hungry subjects surrounded the pot of pasta in the center of their table and dug in. At the end of the meal, a host circulated through the crowd to ensure that the kids had eaten to their heart's delight. All twenty reported feeling well fed and satisfied.

But, despite the fact that they were equally satisfied, not all were treated equally. At one table kids were given nine-inch paper plates to eat from; the kids at the other table were provided with twelve-inch plates. In both cases, most of the subjects went back for more food, and all stopped when they said they were full and wanted no more.

Our goal was to test whether plate size affected how much the subjects ate despite the fact that they could—and did—reload them. Not only did plate size affect consumption—but it affected it a lot. The kids with the large plates ate 70 percent more pasta. Most surprisingly, they didn't know they ate more, nor did they pay much attention to the plate size. Nevertheless, the plate size had an enormous impact on how much it took the kids to get *equally* full.

These junior soccer players aren't the only people who have fallen victim to a large plate. Take a look in your own cupboard. There's a good chance that the dinner plates you'll find there are the same size as your grandmother's *serving platters*. Over the last couple of generations, the plates sold in stores have inched larger without our noticing.

This would probably be no big deal except for the fact that research conducted by eating expert Brian Wansink at Cornell University shows that people eat 92 percent of whatever is on their plate—regardless of how big it is.[1] The difference between twelve-inch and nine-inch plates totals 33 percent more calories! It's little wonder that we're growing larger as a populace. Our plates made us do it!

Of course, this chapter isn't about plates, per se. It's about the entire physical world out there and how it affects our behavior in ways we rarely see. Plates are just one example of how the physical world influences our behavior. The presence or absence of a dining table affects the frequency of a family's interaction. The amount you exercise drops directly with the distance between your TV and your exercise equipment... you get the idea. *Things* quietly affect all of our choices—and our bad habits are hardly immune.

For instance, Katie B. struggled to stay up-to-date in her field. To make sure that she didn't slide into a career slump, she stacked piles of professional journals next to her reading chair. Unfortunately, her home was not designed for reading. It was designed for viewing. Katie's fifty-inch flat-screen stood like an altar in the center of her living room. Her DVR recorded fascinating fare for any occasion or mood. The surround-sound speakers made her feel as if she were in the middle of the action. It was like living in a movie theater.

So when Katie arrived home at six thirty every night, the living room she had so carefully outfitted conspired against her best intentions to read journals. It was as if she had purposely plotted against her own wishes—while in truth, Katie had given no thought to the fact that the way she was constructing her physical space was undermining her career.

It seems most people are not thinking about how their home's design affects their family's behavior. Today's consumers often buy nifty new devices because they can, not necessarily because they'll help them achieve their family goals. And guess what the results have been. Supply your home with four different video platforms, populate them with dozens of exciting video games, add a home theater complete with several comfortable couches, and—voilà—you've compiled the perfect recipe for childhood obesity.

How about the impact of *things* on a problem such as drug abuse?

Changer Wes M. woefully underestimated the roles things in his environment were playing in his cocaine addiction. The mild-mannered accountant from San Diego was highly motivated to get off drugs—but he also had a Facebook account and owned an iPhone, and both were working against him.

After five disappointing relapses, Wes began to realize that he wasn't a match for his digital foes. He would be toeing the line, and then a tantalizing text message from an old accomplice would tempt him to use drugs, or perhaps he'd receive a Facebook invitation to a party he just couldn't miss.

These alluring electronic reminders were often more than Wes could resist. Technology was bringing temptations closer and more frequently than he had the will to overcome. His physical surroundings lay in wait for him so that at any moment when his personal motivation flagged, his fall would be *inevitable*. Wes continued to struggle until he eventually made a digital overhaul.

You live in that same powerful physical world. Every single day of your life you face opponents that are always around you, never sleep, are completely unyielding, and are so quiet that you stop noticing they're even there. Such is the power of *things*. So, if you ever hope to take control of your life, you'll have to first take control of your space.

The good news is that when you do, you gain the same sleepless ally supporting your change effort. Your job is to find the subtle ways your personal environment currently enables your old habits and then redesign it to support your new ones. When you transform your environment from foe into friend, you can make the changes that sometimes feel impossible practically inevitable.

TACTIC 1: BUILD FENCES

According to historians, it took fences to tame the Wild West (good news if you're the tamer, bad news if you're the tamed). When it comes to your own wild world filled with enticing temptations and dangerous consequences, you'll need to build some fences as well. Of course, the fences we're talking about aren't barbed-wired barriers; they're simply boundaries you create in your life. They come in the form of intractable rules and decisive actions that keep you out of harm's way. These personal fences make it easier for you to stand up to certain threats.

For example, when Michael V. got serious about sobriety, he put a fence around the most dangerous, tempting places in his environment.

"I made a rule about the route I took home from work," Michael explains. "I would never drive by Toni's, my favorite bar. I knew if I drove by that bar, chances were good I'd see a friend's car in the parking lot, and I'd be tempted to stop. So I stopped driving by Toni's."

In fact, Michael put a fence around all bars.

"Why would I go into a bar," Michael continues, "except to drink? I don't need to be in a bar."

Further, Michael put a fence around his home. "I no longer keep any alcohol in my home. I don't need it calling out to me."

These intractable rules made his personal environment safer by fencing out the bad stuff. Michael used fences to create an environment he could master.

Consider the following financial fitness example. When June W. needed to get her debt under control (at one point the interest payments on her debt matched her rent payment), she built several fences that protected her from uncontrolled spending. First June cut up her credit cards. This decisive action made it impossible for her to go into credit card debt, period. She also made all visits to malls off limits unless she had a list of specific items she would buy. Her list limited her to planned spending and fenced off any impulse buying.

Katie B., the woman who wanted to read work-related journals (but then built a veritable temple for watching TV), used a fence to help change her evening habits as well. She moved all of her digital temptations to the spare room in her apartment so that the path of least resistance was to pick up a professional journal and study up on her career rather than plop in her chair and veg out. She still enjoyed some TV time in the evening—but she had to "hop the fence" to get to the TV and DVR, which made it an intentional rather than a default activity.

Fences can be quite helpful, but they can also create unintended problems if you don't prepare for a world without them. If you're only successful when fences make bad choices impossible, you might not fare so well when the fences come down.

Here's the problem: Fences work so well that we often rely on them as our sole solution. We put criminals behind bars; we send addicts to rehab; and some overeaters even wire their mouths shut. These fences work fine as long as they are maintained, but most criminals, addicts, and overeaters eventually leave these fences behind. Then old problems recur, and if those who needed the fences in the first place have made no other changes, they immediately fall prey to their old habits.

Two rules of thumb can help keep fences functional.

Make Sure You're the One Who Builds and Maintains the Fence.
The decision to fence off a temptation should be yours. It's not the choice of your friends, co-workers, loved ones, or family—no matter how well intended. Michael V. talked about the early days when his family and friends tried to get him to make bars out of bounds. Unfortunately, since it wasn't his decision, he experienced their fences as meddling. The fence became a challenge rather than a tool—so he spent his time finding ways around it rather than benefiting from its protection. Create your own fences by asking yourself what you really want and then putting up barriers that help you achieve it

Don't Use a Fence in Place of a Six-Source Plan. Some people find such comfort in fences that they end up relying on them exclusively. For example, a rehab facility can protect you from bad choices for a few weeks or months, but eventually you'll need to manage these temptations outside the walls of the facility. Supplement the fences. Use the fenced-off rehab facility to build delay-of-gratification and other sobriety skills, but then add other six-source tactics that will assist you in the real world. Otherwise, when the fence comes down ... be prepared for a disappointing crash.

TACTIC 2: MANAGE DISTANCE

Ricardo N. had to change his schedule to save his marriage. He and his wife, Helen, lived on opposite ends of the day. She would leave for work at five a.m. and return just as he was taking off at three p.m. And they wondered why they were drifting apart—despite a variety of heartfelt efforts to relight their flame.

When Ricardo eventually changed jobs after a new opportunity arose—a job that coincided with his wife's schedule—he quickly learned that all of his attempts to improve their relationship paled in comparison to the simple act of creating more time together. He discovered that he had to increase their proximity before they could improve their intimacy. Distance affects behavior.

When it comes to distance, it's not just about love. For example, consider Changer Liz P. Her workstation sat only fifteen feet away from what she and her co-workers referred to as "the trough"—a large metal bin that was always stocked with candy. Liz and her colleagues engaged in ritual feeding from it every day. The trough quietly sat there and played the role of siren seductress as Liz fought the battle of adhering to a balanced diet.

But one day Liz began to see how the physical world was acting on her and decided to take charge of her surroundings. Rather than put up a fence by making it a rule not to eat from the trough (a rule she might find hard to follow), Liz took a different approach. She asked to be moved to an empty workstation fifty feet away from the trough, and a week later, when her request was granted, she dropped her candy consumption altogether. By changing work spaces, Liz was adhering to the adage

Keep good things close and convenient,
and bad things distant and difficult.

Okay, maybe this expression isn't exactly an adage, but when it comes to Source 6, it should be. If you can create a distance between yourself and temptation, do so. You can stare in the face of temptation and try to tough it out—stepping once again into the willpower trap—or you can use distance to your advantage. Choose distance every time.

But was fifty feet really a large enough distance to make a difference for Liz? Psychologists study the role physical distance plays in our choices, and they'd be the first to say that moving a temptation just a few feet one way or another can have a huge impact on one's behavior. For instance, if you finish half your meal at a restaurant and sit there with the plate in front of you while you talk to your friends, twenty minutes later your plate will be empty. Move the half-full plate six feet away to the other corner of the table, and it'll remain half full.

Here are just a few of the curious effects distance can play in one's life outside a restaurant: It is one of the best predictors of friendship and love; it predicts scientific collaboration; and it largely accounts for one's leisure-time activities.

It turns out that humans are far more governed by distance than anyone would guess. Here's how you can use it to your advantage.

If you want to exercise more, keep workout equipment conveniently close in your bedroom or living room, not in the basement or a distant gym.

If you want to quit or cut back on smoking, place your supply in a distant room and up on a shelf—or banish it altogether.

If you want to reduce spending, remove Internet bookmarks for all of your shopping pages. Just a little electronic distance can change your spending habits. You get the idea. Turn space from the final frontier into your change ally.

TACTIC 3: CHANGE CUES

Like it or not, your environment can have a huge impact on what gets your attention. Signs, colors, shapes, sounds—anything that might grab your attention—can affect your opinions, emotions, and choices. Remember the kids in our Change Anything Labs spending study in the chapter "Escape the Willpower Trap"? When our subjects entered a lab with bare walls, they saved an average of $6.22 in the first round. But when, in addition to a couple of other small changes, they faced four colorful posters of tasty treats, their savings plummeted to $3.23. The kids scarcely remembered the signs, but the subtle visual cues appeared to have an impact.

Visual and other cues help set your mental agenda. They tell you what to think about, what to worry about, and what to want. In fact, Stephen Hoch of the Wharton School of the University of Pennsylvania suggests that one reason visual cues are so powerful is that they turn things from a "want" into a "need." When you see something you had not formerly been thinking about, you are suddenly reminded that you don't have it—which creates a sense of dissatisfaction.[2]

Think of it this way: Before you saw the new mobile phone features, you were perfectly happy with the phone you had. But after seeing the full-page ad about the latest model, your phone seems outdated and frumpy. You want—no, you *need*—to be current and not frumpy. That's right; you don't just want that new phone. You *need* it.

It's time to get these same cues pushing your wants and needs in the right direction. Take charge of what catches your attention by giving yourself little wake-up calls at crucial moments. Use cues to remind yourself of your resolutions in the very moments you're most likely to forget.

The best cues are the ones that kick you off autopilot and remind you of the commitments you've made and the results you want to achieve.

They also suggest an immediate next step. For instance, June W., who was trying to reduce her debt, used a cell phone application that asked her periodically to input how much she had spent. It then tallied up her budget standings and let her know whether she was over or under budget for the week and month. Just this small regular nudge and a cue about her "score" made June far more mindful of her choices and changed her habits almost immediately.

Maria O. cued herself to practice her vital behaviors for improving her relationship with her life partner by simply putting what she called a "preflight checklist" on the dashboard of her car. After a stressful day at work, the card would remind her to pause; take four deep breaths; recall one reason she adored her life partner; then enter the house with a smile. Like a pilot, she found that if she went through her checklist before taking off, things went a lot more smoothly each evening.

At work, cues can also play an important role in keeping you on track. For instance, individuals who attend leadership training courses often hang up posters summarizing the skills they just learned to remind them that when faced with new challenges, they need to implement the skills rather than fall into their former habits.

To cue themselves not to be angry when addressing a problem with a direct report (a mistake they had often made before and that had caused them no end of problems), one group of leaders we worked with placed mirrors in their workstations. When they heard about a problem that needed to be addressed, they stood and walked to their cubicle doors, but before they exited they looked in the mirror to ensure that they weren't entering the upcoming conversation feeling angry—or at least looking angry. If an angry person looked back at them from the mirror, they took a deep breath and practiced the anger-management techniques they had learned.

Still another group we worked with placed small orange circles at locations where they tended to feel stress (certain meeting rooms, their steering wheel, and so forth). The colored circles served as cues to remind them to employ the stress-reduction tactics they had learned at a recent seminar.

Laura A. created an interesting physical cue that helped her become more mindful of her tendency to be critical of friends and family and replace it with a habit of building others up. When she would hear herself say something hurtful, she would open and close her right hand three times. When she made a supportive comment, she would open and close her left hand three times. Over the course of a week, she found she was far more mindful of the comments she would make and well on her way to changing her words and her relationships.

Some of the best cues are scorecards you can place in prominent locations to keep your progress at the forefront of your mind. Of course, these days some come in the form of electronic mobile phone applications. But Scott H. found that simply placing a checkmark on an old-fashioned wall calendar every day he practiced his vital behaviors was enough to keep them at the forefront of his mind.

One important thing to remember about cues is that many of them have a half-life. Over time they become one more invisible part of your environment, so they stop working. The solution is to conduct a regular environmental audit. Conduct a review of your home, your car, your neighborhood, and your workplace and look for places where cues would help you stay on track. Then create little reminders, not so obvious that they're embarrassing, but obvious enough to grab your attention. As you repeat this process, you'll discover that your crucial moments change over time. Creating new cues is a powerful way of taking charge of your space.

TACTIC 4: ENGAGE YOUR AUTOPILOT

It turns out that you can actually make laziness a tool in your change arsenal. For decades, social scientists have demonstrated that we humans have a *default bias*. That's a nice way of saying we would rather not mess with things once they're arranged. Once you get comfortable with a certain aspect of your life, say, the route you drive to work, you don't easily make changes. Once you've picked a path that seems to work, you follow it for decades—even if a better one surfaces. You save your brain capacity for heftier challenges—such as the meaning of life or figuring out whether the guy ahead of you in the ten-items-or-less line actually has twelve items.

For example, economics professor Anna Breman asked donors to a large charity if they would be willing to donate more to their worthy cause. Everyone *wanted* to but few would agree to do it *today*. So instead, she offered them the option of putting small monthly increases on autopilot in the coming months. Once people set up this default condition, most let it run—increasing their donations by 32 percent over time![3]

How can this proclivity be turned in your favor? By setting up positive defaults in your life. You can set things on autopilot and then count on your tendency to go with the flow to structurally enable you to make better choices. For example, Steve and Tina G. noticed they were drifting apart, so they created an autopilot to bring them back together: They bought season tickets to a local theater and placed dates on their calendar for the next six months. The default condition was now that they would have a date. It would take an active effort to cancel it. This couple who had struggled to find time together made it to every one of the six performances ... together.

You can set autopilots for yourself by using standing appointments, automatic withdrawals, long-term subscriptions—and any other mechanism that takes advantage of your desire to avoid thinking.

TACTIC 5: USE TOOLS

How would you like to join an extraordinarily successful health club? It's made up of people who are rarely obese (around 4 percent), and yet they consume heaping mounds of meat, potatoes, gravy, eggs, vegetables, bread, pies, cakes—all oozing in fat and refined sugar. What's the group's secret? Well, on a slow day they walk well over ten thousand steps and the other six days of the week they put in huge amounts of exercise. Which, of course, leads to the question, How do these folks get themselves to do all that?

Did we mention that the group also spurns modern contrivances such as automobiles, blenders, mobile phones, and the like? By now you've perhaps guessed that the "club" we're referring to is made up of the Amish,[4] and they make our next point for us. Many of the tools we've created to make our lives easier have landed us in the fix we're currently in.

For instance, it requires virtually dozens of contraptions to keep us stationary most of the day, and most of us have access to every single

one of them. It has taken more than a century of culinary analysis
to produce amazingly unhealthful foods that a child can nuke in
seconds—and many do. TV sets strategically positioned in nearly every
person's bedroom can isolate individuals to the point where conversation
becomes a rarity. According to the latest Nielsen study, the average American spends about seven hours a day using some type of media. Television
alone counts for four hours a day during which the average child views
twenty thousand advertisements a year and two hundred thousand acts
of violence by the time he or she is eighteen.[5] It's a wonder we're not all
350-pound, bankrupt, divorced ax murderers.

But what if we took these same tools and used them to our advantage? That's exactly what many of the Changers we studied did. For
example, as several lost weight, they made use of an electronic device
that displayed their current calorie burn rate along with total steps and
calories per day.

"It was amazing," exclaimed Rod M., one of our Changers. "I could
see in real time the impact my activity was having on my calorie burn.
Plus seeing how increasing my effort on the treadmill also increased my
caloric burn rate was a big motivator."

The chances for making good use of tools only increase with each
new invention. For instance, the Internet can provide a social network for
both motivating and enabling your change as well as dozens of tools for
tracking and broadcasting your efforts. With new advances in software,
you're able to track your budget by category—at the very moment you're
spending.[6] Cuing devices planted into your computer can remind you to
do everything from walking for five minutes every hour to stepping up to
a crucial conversation with your boss.

Or you can go old school. For instance, if you want to increase family unity, change how you use the microwave oven. This revolutionary, time-saving device can turn a family of four into four separate individuals who make their own quick meals, at their own times, which they then eat by themselves in front of a TV or game module. But if an entire family were to sit down to eat at a family table...[7]

Speaking of furniture, Ricardo N. reports that a porch swing helped save his marriage. He and his wife, Helen, went through a troubled time after they aligned their jobs. They now had time to spend together but had fallen into the habit of winding down after work by plopping in front of a TV (he in the den, she in the family room) and then settling into a solitary activity of some sort. They just weren't used to spending time together.

Enter the porch swing. Ricardo and Helen committed to sit for fifteen minutes and just talk about their day and any concerns they wanted to air. To signal their commitment, they bought the porch swing and designated it as the location for their nightly parleys. The swing served as a cue that reminded them of their agreement, and it also offered an attractive and comfortable place that made talking less stressful. Finally, it had an unanticipated positive effect. Somehow sitting side by side in the confined space created a warmth that soothed their emotions and made understanding come easier. Less physical distance led to less emotional distance.

SUMMARY: CONTROL YOUR SPACE

As we've studied how Changers have succeeded at overcoming the pull of the past, we've learned that all use things to make new habits practically inevitable. You should take advantage of the same resources.

Build Fences. What rules should you set to keep you acting in healthy ways? What decisive actions, if routinely taken, would keep you out of harm's way? Remember, don't use these fences as a sole source for change, and don't let anyone else set them up for you. Create your own rules, and use them in conjunction with the five other sources of influence.

Manage Distance. What are you doing to keep good things close and convenient and bad things distant and difficult? Have you thought about moving tempting items away from the places you work and rest? It won't require miles or even blocks; sometimes a few feet one way or the other will be all it takes.

Change Cues. Are there places you can put up reminders that will help keep you on track? Think of your crucial moments; if they come at predictable places, you can post reminders to stay true to your plan. If they come at predictable times or events, you can have them appear on your computer or phone—just before the event, as a timely reminder.

Engage Your Autopilot. Are there standing commitments you can make that will make positive change the path of least resistance? The more you structure good choices as the default in your life, the easier change becomes.

Use Tools. Speaking of your computer and phone, what are you doing to transform electronic devices and other tools into valuable change allies? How is everything from your TV to your phone to your computer currently conspiring against your plan to improve? What can you do to transform this silent enemy into a genuine tool for change?

While we're on the topic of using tools to assist your change effort, don't forget to log in to ChangeAnything.com and see how people just like you have found ways to use fences, distance, cues, and tools to control their space.

PART III

HOW TO CHANGE ANYTHING

The following five chapters provide context for the material we've covered so far. They are not intended as stand-alone career, wellness, addiction, or other self-help pieces, but as vibrant, living examples of how the science of personal success can be applied to common problems. Each chapter starts by identifying vital behaviors that research shows typically help individuals overcome their challenges (although even these vary by person) and then tracks how a few Changers applied the ideas and tactics we've shared to everything from sagging careers, to growing addictions, to failing relationships.

The goal of each of these application chapters is not to provide a list of actions that you should take, but to demonstrate how others have used the ideas to their advantage. As we explained earlier, you will need to tailor the vital behaviors to your crucial moments and the six-source strategies to your vital behaviors. When it comes to your personal change plan, you'll still need to be the scientist and the subject. Nevertheless, by providing you with examples of what real people have done with five widely shared problems, we hope to provide added insights into how you can use the new science of personal success to your advantage.

Career

How to Get
Unstuck at Work

Let's start this chapter with a rather surprising research finding uncovered at the Change Anything Labs. A whopping 87 percent of the folks we surveyed say they have bosses who've prevented them from getting the pay, promotions, or other opportunities they wanted because of a concern they've had about their performance.[1]

From within this same population, close to half of the respondents also believe they are in the top 10 percent of performers in their company. So it's easy to understand why more than two-thirds of these employees have been surprised by the negative things their managers have said about them in a performance review. They believe in themselves and their accomplishments, but their bosses have a far less rosy view.

Now, if the fact that your boss doesn't always think you're among the tip-top performers were merely a statistic without consequences, then the idea that your boss undervalues you would just be annoying. But if as a result of that view, your boss doesn't give you, say, the 2 percent raise that is being offered to a select few employees—and if you're thirty years old, earning $60,000 per year, this loss of a 2 percent raise adds up over your career to $59,780. And if, heaven forbid, you were denied a promotion you deserved, over your career this could cost you more than $250,000.

In addition to taking a financial hit, what happens to morale and work effort when people who think they are solid performers feel they're underappreciated and under-rewarded? According to sociologist Daniel Yankelovich, *discretionary effort* takes a real hit. That is, the gap between how much energy, effort, and creativity an employee is offering today and how much the employee *could* give your firm if he or she so desired is surprisingly large. More than two-thirds of employees report that they have much more discretionary contribution than they currently give.[2] In one study we conducted at the Change Anything Labs, more than half of the employees we surveyed suggested that when it came to effort at work, they did the least amount possible without getting fired.[3]

So, what's a person to do? You think you're doing well; your boss holds a less enthusiastic opinion. Or you think you're a top 5 percent performer and your boss puts you in the top 30 percent. Either way, this gap in appreciation is costing you money, it can be a real drain on your morale, and both you and the company are suffering. What will it take to get others thinking what you think and get your career back on track?

To see what it takes to turn a career around, we'll follow the story of one of our Changers, Melanie R. Like many hardworking people, she was always able to figure out how to get ahead. She waited tables to put herself through college and took night bookkeeping jobs to pay for her MBA. But now, six years into her career, she's stuck. She's just learned she's been passed over for a key job assignment—for the second time.

Melanie knows she's one of the smartest and most productive people on her team. But in spite of her tireless effort, she seems to be spinning her wheels. In fact, if she can't get her career on track, she'll be at risk of being pushed out of the firm. What does she need to do to get her career back on track?

To answer this oft-asked question, we'll look at research into the common behaviors of top-ranked performers. These are the folks out there who are getting the bonuses, plush assignments, and promotions. What are they doing that others aren't?

WHAT SEPARATES THE BEST FROM THE REST?

Over the past couple of decades we've studied the most influential and respected employees in more than fifty companies and dozens of industries. We entered organizations and asked thousands of employees (including the bosses) to give us the names of the three people whose opinions, work, and abilities they most admired. We wanted to find the go-to people—and we did.

When we looked closely at these highly valued individuals, we soon learned that they hadn't been singled out because of a popularity contest. Rather, they had won a productivity contest. They weren't politicians; they were valued resources.

Next came the real work. We had to uncover what these high performers did that made them so valued—by peers and bosses alike. Here is what we found. Across organizations as different as sawmills, government agencies, tech start-ups, and charitable nonprofits, *top performers practice the same three vital behaviors*

1. Know Your Stuff. Okay, we admit, this sounds a bit vague, so let's clarify what we mean by "stuff." Top performers put regular effort into ensuring that they are good at the technical aspects of their jobs. If their job is to sort lumber, they fall asleep at night pondering sorting strategies. If they're in marketing, then they voraciously acquire the best marketing knowledge available. You get the picture. They work hard at honing their craft.

2. Focus on the Right Stuff. In addition to performing their craft well, top performers contribute to tasks that are essential to the organization's success. This is important to grasp. Not all contributions are equal. Highly valued employees help manage what Stanford University's Jeffrey Pfeffer calls the company's "critical uncertainties."[4] If a company is having trouble manufacturing its product, top performers find a way to help resolve that problem. If the firm is fighting legal challenges, top performers apply their specific expertise to that issue. If nobody has figured out how to market the product, top performers are hip deep in solving that problem.

And how do top performers get these mission-critical assignments? First, they are intensely interested in understanding where the organization is going (with emphasis on the key challenges). They study their own company. Next (and this is their true genius) they equip themselves to make their best and highest contribution to the core elements of where their company is going. Top performers work on their skill set and their access to critical tasks.

3. Build a Reputation for Being Helpful. But doing your job well and ensuring that you're helping deal with the company's most important challenges isn't enough. It's necessary but insufficient. Individuals who are singled out by their colleagues as the go-to folks in the company are also widely known across their teams and sometimes even their entire organizations. They are far more likely than average to be recognized by name, and, more importantly, *people describe them as experts who are generous with their time.*

Taking time to help their co-workers puts top performers at the hub of important networks. Take note: This is not your typical networking observation. Top performers don't get to know people simply to build an impressive collection of business cards. Theirs is not primarily a self-serving motivation. Top people are widely known and respected by others not because of their frequent contact, charm, or likability, but because *they help others solve their problems.*

FIND *YOUR* VITAL BEHAVIORS

Now that you know what it takes to be a highly valued employee in general, you'll need to tailor these three generic vital behaviors to your specific circumstances. For instance, what aspects of your job do you really need to nail? You have what's written on your job description, but does this document cover some of the more subtle, yet essential, components of your job that distinguish top performers from the multitude in the middle-performing ranks? Next, what are the "critical uncertainties" in your company, and how do you even find them? Finally, who exactly should know you and see you as being helpful?

To answer these questions, let's return to Melanie, our accountant who felt stuck in her career. In spite of her energy and intelligence, she was at risk of being dropped at the next reduction in force.

Melanie began by measuring herself against the three career vital behaviors. She asked, "Do I know my stuff?" "Do I focus on the right stuff?" and "Do others see me as helpful?" But she didn't ask just herself these questions; she sat down with her boss and asked him as well. He took a bit of coaxing, but as he sensed Melanie's sincerity, he began to open up. Here is what he had to say.

"Melanie, you came here as a good accountant. Your grades were right in line with what we want, but you've kind of sidetracked yourself. You've volunteered for a couple of big HR projects, and that reduced your billable hours."

Melanie had been *working on the wrong stuff.* She was spending too much time on something that interested *her* as opposed to what was important to the organization. She was lagging in billable hours, and none of the other contributions she made could make up for that. So, she volunteered to work on a major account where she could rack up some serious time. And she was turned down flat.

Melanie made a lunch appointment with Tara, the manager who had turned her down, and learned two more important bits of information. First, Tara didn't want anyone on her team who hadn't already been "bloodied" at another major account. She told Melanie that she needed to prove herself with a tough and demanding client before coming to work on her team.

Second, Tara looked at Melanie's HR assignments as evidence that she wasn't up nights studying ongoing revisions to tax law—and she was right about that. Melanie had been working long days and weekends trying to complete the HR projects and still maintain her billable hours. She hadn't been using her extra hours to study tax law. And now she was behind. She didn't *know her stuff* the way she should.

At this point Melanie was a bit disappointed, but at least she knew where she stood on the three vital behaviors:

- She no longer knew her stuff well enough. She needed to skill up on tax law.
- She hadn't been working on the right stuff. She needed to boost her billable hours.
- She wasn't viewed as helping out on tough jobs because she had never been assigned to a major account. She needed to prove herself with an especially demanding customer.

APPLY SIX-SOURCE STRATEGIES

Now, what will it take for Melanie to turn her vital behaviors into vital habits? Mastering tax law meant taking a company-sponsored seminar that met twice a week. It also meant she'd have to do an hour of tough homework every night. Building her billable hours meant giving up lots of personal time and agreeing to travel almost every week. The demanding customer would come naturally if she worked the billable hours she planned.

As we now know, Melanie has no hope of turning these behaviors into habits unless she is both motivated *and* able to do so. So she started with a gut check for motivation. Melanie's first question was, "Is it worth it?" Her immediate answer was, "Absolutely!" She had already invested in a college education and a master's degree. Getting her career on track would mean she could double her salary in the next five years. Failing would mean disgrace in her own eyes.

With this in mind, Melanie was realistic about the barriers she'd face in changing her own behavior. The extensive study and travel were going to take some adjustment. She knew it would take more than a motivating moment to stay on track and achieve her goals. So she created a six-source plan to influence her own behavior. The plan included several tactics from each of the six sources.

SOURCE 1: LOVE WHAT YOU HATE

The real challenge to Melanie's personal motivation came when she had to put her TV away in a closet, sell her season basketball tickets, and stay after work and study tax law. These enticing distractions made up her crucial moments, or times when she was most tempted to toss her plans out the window. At these moments, when Melanie was at her weakest, she really needed to focus on her long-term future rather than her fleeting pleasures. She had to find a way to make the distant and murky future more salient, plausible, and compelling.

To get started, Melanie *told the whole vivid story.* She examined each step in her career and what each would really mean to her. Then it hit her. Melanie had taken a picture of a beautiful vacation home she had stayed at during a company retreat a few years back and decided that one day she'd own one just like it. So she put the picture next to her computer to remind herself when she sat down to study each night of what she might enjoy one day if she stuck to her guns.

Next, rather than beat herself into doing work when she didn't feel like it, Melanie made a rule that she could choose to slack off—but only after reciting a *Personal Motivation Statement* she carried on the screen of her mobile phone. Notice how Melanie *used value words*: "I'd like to see myself as a talented contributor. I'd like to increase my income so I can buy a house. I'd like to have the respect and admiration of the smartest people in our company."

After slowly reading this statement, more often than not Melanie felt more motivated to set aside the present for an even better future. She rarely slacked off when she used this tactic.

Next, in order to love what she hated, Melanie *visited her default future* by taking a hard look at several co-workers who had leveled out early in their careers and worked the same job for a couple of decades— without promotions or real pay increases. She took time to imagine exactly what her life would be like if she followed the same path.

As Melanie continued shaping her new habits, she set up an automatic e-mail to arrive in her inbox on days when she expected to struggle the most to keep on task. The e-mail contained the organizational announcement of those who were promoted the last time she was passed over. Seeing her name missing on the e-mail list reminded Melanie of the future she would continue to face if she let herself get distracted.

Finally, Melanie made the whole process a personal competition by keeping a score of her billable hours and posting them on a big poster in her living room. She *made a game* out of trying to increase the numbers every week.

These tailored-to-Melanie tactics became her way of learning to love what she hated. Whenever Melanie felt dispirited, bored, or exhausted with the demanding plan she had created for herself, she would run through these motivators, and they would help her persevere.

SOURCE 2: DO WHAT YOU CAN'T

When Melanie originally searched for her vital behaviors, she *completed a skill scan*. After learning what she needed to be good at in order to succeed at work, she decided to become an expert in the new tax laws. She figured she could master these laws in a few months.

Melanie then attended a company-sponsored tax-law seminar and volunteered to take notes for others who couldn't attend. After she wrote up her notes, she met with the instructor to make sure they were accurate.

Melanie quickly learned the value of *deliberate practice*. At first she took notes, studied more, and then took more notes—but it didn't take long until she realized that she needed to apply what she had learned, and then get feedback from an expert. Otherwise, she was going to forget everything. So Melanie wrote recommendations for each of her clients (based on the new tax laws) and asked her manager and the course instructor to review them. They gave her feedback, and she quickly made changes. Melanie then repeated the process with the clients.

In a matter of a couple of weeks, perceptions of Melanie began to change. People appreciated her willingness to pass on her new-found skills to them. She was surprised at how quickly people had softened what she thought had been deeply entrenched attitudes about her.

SOURCES 3 AND 4: TURN ACCOMPLICES INTO FRIENDS

In order to make use of social motivators and enablers, Melanie held a *transformation conversation* by talking to Tony, her life partner, to make sure the extra work involved in getting her career back on track would fit into both their long-term aspirations and their daily life. Historically Tony had been an enabler—encouraging Melanie to "carpe diem" and not do so much at work. But after hearing Melanie's goals and plan, Tony agreed to support her by encouraging her to take classes and do homework—rather than tempting her with entertainment options. The two of them also agreed to opt out of their softball league for the year.

Melanie took additional steps to ensure that when it came to her new plan, her boss would be a friend—and not an accomplice to her old work habits. He had hired her and wanted to see her succeed. She met with him every two weeks to keep him updated and to make sure she was pursuing his priorities. She was careful not to appear insecure with constant demands for attention—but used these modest check-ins to synchronize with his priorities.

Melanie also *added new friends* by connecting with two people from the tax-law seminar. The three pooled their notes, shared insights, quizzed each other, and encouraged one another to keep on track. Before each lecture they called each other, talked about what they had read, and ensured that they would be attending class.

SOURCE 5: INVERT THE ECONOMY

To make use of financial incentives, Melanie placed some of her own hard-earned cash at risk and then asked Tony to be her referee. Melanie put ten twenty-dollar bills in a jar. Every Friday, if Tony agreed that she had made her goal for the week, she took one of the twenty-dollar bills out of the first jar and put it in a second jar, labeled "New Bicycle." If she didn't make the goal, she had to put the twenty-dollar bill into a jar labeled with the name of the political party she opposed. At the end of ten weeks, Melanie had made every career advancement goal and had $160 to put toward a new bicycle. And she'd sent only forty dollars to her least-favorite political party.

SOURCE 6: CONTROL YOUR SPACE

Melanie made her new habits easier to practice by enlisting the help of her physical surroundings as well. First, she *used cues*. As described earlier, she positioned a photo of her vacation home next to her computer, she placed a motivational message on her cell-phone screen, and she e-mailed herself the promotion announcement that was conspicuously missing her name.

Melanie also *built fences*. Rather than face the temptation of cutting class and going to a basketball game—consistently for an entire season—Melanie sold her tickets. No use revisiting that choice over and over again. She also made a firm rule that it would be okay to slack off from her plan, but only after she read her Personal Motivation Statement.

Melanie *used tools*. She audited her calendar and found that two of her smaller customers were taking up more of her time than they should—causing her to spend too little time with her larger customers. So Melanie set up a plan to touch base with her key customers every week and decided how she would throttle back with the smaller customers.

Melanie also set aside an hour every day after work to study her course work. She found she had to structure this time into her schedule in advance or it just never happened. She made a recurring to-do reminder in her calendar that beeped and buzzed until she scheduled her next study session.

YOUR PLAN FOR GETTING UNSTUCK

Our Changer Melanie R. was eventually successful in getting that next promotion, but only after she studied the three career vital behaviors. She asked herself: "Do I know my stuff?" "Do I focus on the right stuff?" and "Do others see me as helpful?" To answer these questions, Melanie talked with her boss and other key people and discussed how each high-leverage action applied to her particular career. From there Melanie created her own vital behaviors along with a six-source plan to keep her on track. No single tactic

kept Melanie motivated and able, but when she used them in combination she learned what worked and what didn't and eventually
succeeded.

Before you work up your own plan, let's make sure that your circumstances fit the advice that follows. If you work for a ten-person company,
the three people above you are all owners, and you want to advance, you
don't need career advice; you need a new job.

However, if you have had opportunities to advance but have been
passed over, then read on. If your performance reviews have included
negative surprises, or if you feel like you've been set aside and left to
flounder, or if you believe that the entire promotion and review process
is a mystery, unfair, political, and random, it's time to shine a light on
what's really going on and to take your career in your own hands.

FIND YOUR VITAL BEHAVIORS

With some personal problems such as smoking, using harmful drugs, or
spending in excess, the vital behaviors you need to enact are clear—stop
doing what's bad for you. It may not be easy to stop, but at least you know
what to do. With career challenges, though, it can take some work to
tease out the unique behaviors you'll have to bring into play in order to
get unstuck.

Earlier we mentioned that Melanie talked to her boss about her
vital behaviors. For Melanie, it took some coaxing, but her boss finally
explained to her exactly what he thought Melanie needed to do. Let's take
a look at what "coaxing" can look like. It can be challenging.

Let's say you've explained to your boss that you want to be a valuable asset to the company and are seeking advice on what you should
do to improve your chances of advancement. Or perhaps you're trying

to respond to recent concerns your boss expressed during a performance review.

In either case, your boss explains that your problem is that you're not a very good "team player." He seems earnest enough and believes that he's given you valuable advice. In truth, you don't know what your boss means. So you ask him what being a team player actually entails. He pauses for a second, takes a deep breath, and then explains that you need to be "easier to approach." This has you curious. Since when have you been hard to approach? What does that even mean?

The problem here is that you're looking for behaviors you need to enact, and your boss (like most people) isn't very good at describing them. First he describes a quality or characteristic—the kind of things you find at the top of a performance review form. He says you need to be a "team player." Qualities such as these are not behaviors and don't tell you what to do.

Second, your boss describes a result. According to him you need to do *something* (and this is what you're trying to discover in the first place) so that others will think you're easy to approach. In this case your boss has told you what to achieve, not what to do. He just thinks he's told you what to do. This type of advice is akin to a coach who tells you that you need to "score more points."

Results masked as behavioral advice are typically nothing more than a painful reminder of the blindingly obvious. In either case, whether people are describing vague qualities or obvious results, you must stick with the conversation until the person advising you identifies the specific actions you need to take in order to know your stuff, do the right stuff, or gain a reputation for being helpful.

To get at your vital behaviors, ask for the latest example of the problem you're trying to solve. Ask what you did or didn't do. Probe for your specific action until the behavior becomes obvious. If you don't identify behaviors, you certainly won't have found your vital behaviors.

There's a second problem with finding your vital behaviors. In the previous example, individuals were unable to give you a behavior description because they confused results and qualities with behaviors. But sometimes the people you talk with don't want to tell you what you need to do to improve. They fear that the feedback will be too embarrassing or insulting, so they hide the truth.

This problem calls for a confidant. As you're trying to find the career vital behaviors you need to enact, include in your search a co-worker who is willing to be frank with you. When it comes to getting feedback, you don't need accomplices who pretend that your current skill set is just dandy. You need honest *coaches* who will tell you where you need to improve.

So, lay out your plan for discovering your vital behaviors. Ask: Do you know your stuff? Do you do the right stuff? Do you have a reputation for being helpful? How are you going to discover where you're coming up short? Whom are you going to talk with, and what will it take for them to describe your vital behaviors?

Weight Loss

How to Lose Weight and
Get Fit—and Stay That Way

OUR GENES ARE STACKED AGAINST US

When you talk to people who have long struggled with the challenge of losing weight, they're often very critical of themselves. To quote Justine M., one of our Changers: "It's embarrassing that a chocolate brownie or a piece of bacon can exert such a hold on you. It's food, for crying out loud, not heroin."

And she's right. Food is not heroin. But she's wrong about how challenging it is to bring food under control. According to scientists who venture to rate how difficult various addictions are to break, junk food sits in either first or second position. That's right; food competes with cocaine, alcohol, nicotine, and yes, even heroin.[1]

Think about it. When it comes to physical cravings, you simply can't toy with the substances to which you're attracted. Imagine if you're a two-pack-a-day smoker and your change plan called for you to puff on a cigarette three, four, or five times a day. Tempting yourself would lead to disaster. If you're going to drop a bad habit, you've got to drop the bad habit all the way.

And that's one of the reasons it can be so difficult to lose weight and keep it off. When it comes to eating too much food, you can't go cold turkey. You still have to place in your mouth regularly the very substances you "abuse," and then stop eating while you still crave more.

Why is that? Why does the human body crave sugars and fats in the first place? You'd think the body would crave things that are good for it—say, baby carrots dipped in a fat-free dressing—you know, the stuff early humanoids found in the back of their caves. (Just kidding.)

Thousands of years ago the craving for fats and proteins served our ancestors very well. These cravings propelled them out of their caves and across the savannah in pursuit of game. Unfortunately, those same cravings now put us at a terrible disadvantage as we drive from our sedentary jobs to markets that are chock-full of delicious fats and sugars—already harvested, trapped, and prepared for us.

Then, when we bite into these sugary, fatty foods, they cause the primitive parts of our brains to light up—throwing us into that desperate gorge-now-or-die mode that drives us to consume far more than we know we should.[2] All of this eating would be fine if, similar to our ancestors, we then roamed the savannah for several days hunting or gathering our next meal. But we don't. Our markets are open every single day. *Hunting* is no more taxing than choosing a brand, and *gathering* involves merely toting bags to the trunk of your car.

To make matters worse, the kinds of foods we find in our markets and restaurants are now designed by clever scientists at the molecular level to match our deepest cravings. Foods are "purified" in much the same way as drugs are, so that they can deliver their effects more efficiently to the brain. Our ancestors ate whole grains; we eat white bread. They ate corn; we eat corn syrup. All of this "purification" led Gene-Jack Wang, MD, the chair of the medical department at the U.S. Department of Energy's Brookhaven National Laboratory, to state, "We make our food very similar to cocaine now."[3]

Yikes! No wonder our cravings for food can be so difficult to bring under control. Our world is perfectly designed to get us to eat, eat, eat— but with no counterbalancing call to the gym. Miss this fact and you can easily underplay your cravings for chocolate and fall into the willpower trap. "It's just food," you think to yourself. "Cut back a little here and there—you know, show a little strength of character—and you'll soon be trim and fit!"

AND IT'S KILLING US

Two out of three adults in the United States are now overweight, and other developed countries are catching up fast. For the first time in history, obesity is a greater threat to health worldwide than hunger.[4] And what about those of us who try to escape the force-feeding frenzy? We spend forty billion dollars a year on diets, but nineteen out of twenty of us lose nothing but our money.[5]

Before we get too depressed, let's travel to Stanford University's medical school, where scholars examined the commercial diets people most often use for weight loss. As we saw in the chapter "Be the Scientist and the Subject," these researchers found that every one of the most popular diets "worked."[6] It turns out things aren't so bad after all. We now have carefully crafted plans to help us counteract our inborn cravings.

And now for the not-so-good news—the news you already know—the diets worked only for people who stuck with them, and pretty much nobody did. Bummer.

So the secret to wellness isn't in the diet or exercise program itself. Any approach that causes you to eat less and exercise more will lead to weight loss and improved fitness. Balanced diets and well-crafted exercise plans—along with shortcuts, secret ingredients, and fat-burning gizmos—all work (and work only) if they result in fewer calories ingested and more calories burned. And they work only if you keep them up—because tomorrow you will be eating again. Several times.

So, this chapter isn't about creating novel recipes or new kinds of jumping jacks. Instead we'll help you create a healthy living plan you can live with—forever. If you don't eventually find a way to enjoy both the food you eat and the exercise you choose, you won't stay with it over the long haul. Diets don't work. What works is creating new habits that lead to the results you want for the rest of your life. You have to stop thinking in terms of short-term campaigns and start thinking about the life you're willing to live. And that can change everything for you.

FITNESS VITAL BEHAVIORS

We'll begin by reviewing the common sense of fitness by examining the three vital behaviors that, as reported by thousands who have lost weight and kept it off, are most likely to lead to success. Later we'll look at what you'll need to do—your very own vital behaviors—but for now, answer the following question. What should your change program include if your goal is weight loss and fitness?

1. Before You Begin a Diet or Exercise Program, Assess Your Overall Health. This one everyone knows. Visit with your doctor to make sure your plans are safe, and don't take on too big a challenge all at once. Make sure you're healthy enough to start a weight-loss and fitness program.

2. Eat Better and Eat Less. Most people already know this. Exactly what foods you choose is constantly debated, but one fact isn't. You'll need to eat fewer calories than you burn. There are thousands of diet tips and recipes to consider to help you do this. But let's cut through the fads and keep the simple truth in mind—take in fewer calories than you burn and you'll lose weight.

How you do this will involve customizing a change plan to yourself.

3. Include a Mix of Stretching, Strengthening, and Cardiovascular Activities. These can take a million forms—including walking, vacuuming, taking the stairs, yoga, Pilates, push-ups, sit-ups, and lifting weights. Again, there are thousands of exercise tips and regimens to consider. They may give you ideas for ways to make your exercise more fun and effective and can certainly provide you with a good starting point. Find one or a combination that you can actually enjoy and keep up over the years.

So much for the generic steps. It's now time to tailor a plan to your unique needs and circumstances. All of the popular diet and fitness plans work—if you stick to them. So let's see what it takes to stick.

IDENTIFY YOUR CRUCIAL MOMENTS

1. Flowchart Your Day, Week, or Month. Describe your typical "eating day" in half-hour increments. Then look at patterns over the course of a week or month to see when challenges occur (e.g., when you travel, on weekends). The strategy here is to map the flow of your day and then look for crucial moments or times when problems occur—when you overeat or skip a chance to exercise.

Changer Mary S. was able to drop fifty pounds in eight months. She began tracking her eating day. She woke up to her alarm at seven a.m. and would lie in bed for a few minutes listening to the news, then shower, get dressed, and eat a bowl of whole-grain cereal with a side of fruit in season. That was the first half hour of a typical day. Then, from seven thirty a.m. until eight a.m., she'd quick-walk half a block to the subway, take the subway downtown, and then walk two blocks to her office. So far, so good.

However, as Mary continued mapping, she found she rarely moved from her desk between the hours of eight a.m. and noon and one p.m. and six p.m. And, when she did move, it was either to eat or to sit in a meeting room. So, she added some exercise breaks to her day. Once in the morning and again in the afternoon she'd walk down the stairs, around the block, and back up the stairs to her fifth-floor office. It took her about fifteen minutes each time, for a total of thirty minutes' extra exercise each day.

2. Focus on Temptations, Obstacles, and Excuses (Crucial Moments). Write down all the tasty temptations you've given in to during the last week, and add in the obstacles or excuses you've used to avoid exercising. Then look for patterns. Mary examined her temptations and realized the biggest were hot cinnamon rolls. When she returned home from work she would snack on them. Then, being tired after work was her biggest obstacle and excuse for not exercising. By the time she got home she was physically and emotionally exhausted.

Finding your crucial moments helps you shrink an all-day, every-day kind of problem into an hour-or-two-a-day kind of problem. You can now target the behaviors that get you out of trouble in just those crucial moments. These are your vital behaviors.

CREATE YOUR VITAL BEHAVIORS

Once you've found your crucial moments (and they'll change as you solve certain problems and new ones emerge), create the rules you'll follow during those high-leverage moments. Create the rules now, when you're not being tempted and you're thinking clearly. These rules, or vital behaviors, should spell out exactly what you'll do when faced with a crucial moment. Here are three examples from Mary S.

Mary set herself a baked-goods rule. When baked goods were around, she would stick to fruit or eat a granola bar from her purse—and nothing else.

Mary would go to bed at ten p.m. so she wouldn't be too tired to exercise in the morning.

Often, a vital behavior is the simple reverse of what failure looks like in the crucial moment. If the failure looks like a five-hundred-calorie cinnamon roll, then the vital behavior is to *not* eat it. At other times the vital behavior is one that helps prevent the problem to begin with—such as eating a two-hundred-calorie alternative *before* you start craving the cinnamon roll. If failure is eating too much of the mashed potatoes at dinner, the vital behavior could be eating larger servings of the healthy foods *before* you start in on the potatoes. Filling some of your gastric real estate with the good stuff before the bad stuff moves in can keep you from temptation.

At other times your vital behavior isn't the simple opposite. It calls for an entirely new behavior. In these cases you can discover them using a powerful tool known as *positive deviance*. Find a time when you succeeded against the odds in one of your crucial moments. For instance, if your norm is to snack after work, then focus on a time when you didn't—when you deviated (positively) from the norm. Ask yourself what was different that day, what it was that enabled you to succeed. Were you busy with errands? Had you eaten a different lunch? Were you involved in some activity? Once you discover exactly what you did, you can make doing it a new rule—a new vital behavior.

Here's an example from another Changer, John H. One of John's crucial moments came at Sunday brunch. He couldn't resist piling his platter high with eggs and bacon and sausage and blintzes and hash browns and sometimes even the pickled herring. Then he'd drown it all in Hollandaise sauce. It wasn't pretty and usually sent him home in a stupor. But one Sunday John found himself with a plate that was only moderately filled, and with a tasty selection. What was different? He'd been busy talking with a visiting niece, and his wife, Louise, had filled his plate for him.

At first John felt a bit resentful. Louise clearly hadn't perfected the Leaning Tower of Eggs Benedict the way he had. But after he'd eaten, he felt good—satisfied, not stuffed. It was a positive-deviance moment for John, and he decided to build on it. His vital behavior for the next several Sundays was to ask Louise to please take charge of his plate.

LEARN AND ADJUST

Don't expect to be able to identify all of your crucial moments and vital behaviors at the beginning. Your progress won't follow a straight line. You'll hit binges and setbacks, but treat these challenges the way any scientist would. Examine your failures with curiosity and concern, not self-condemnation. *You'll quickly discover that you learn more from your failures than from your successes.* The times and situations where you fail are your new crucial moments, and each crucial moment you identify becomes a stepping-stone to your success as you create new vital behaviors—tailored to your latest challenge.

For example, you notice that eating at restaurants kills your eating plan. So, decide on new vital behaviors, such as "Always split your order" or "Order just a side." Then track yourself to see how well your new strategy is working. Maybe splitting orders isn't ideal for you because you're often on your own or you find it awkward to ask. If so, then try another rule, such as "Divide your plate in half" or "Eat your vegetables first." Keep at the crucial moment until you've found the vital behavior that works for you. Learn, adjust; learn more, adjust again. Make even your bad days become good data.

Remember, when it comes to personal change, you're both the scientist and the subject. Subjects stumble once in a while. So scientists learn and adjust what their subjects do.

ENGAGE ALL SIX SOURCES OF INFLUENCE

It's time to reorganize your world in such a way that it motivates and enables your new vital behaviors.

SOURCE 1: LOVE WHAT YOU HATE

Here's the motivation challenge you face: Right now, while you're reading this book and thinking your best thoughts, you have plenty of motivation to do the right thing. You think, "No big deal; I'll just tough it out." Unfortunately, later, when temptation strikes, your motivation will weaken, and you'll give in—overeating, eating the wrong foods, or ducking a chance to exercise. Human beings are simply horrible at predicting how challenging a future temptation will feel, even when they've faced it over and over for years.[7]

To overcome this motivational mistake, learn how to tap into your existing personal motivation—especially in times of intense temptation.

1. Find What You Love. This obvious tactic is frequently overlooked because people can't conceive of the fact that eating healthy and exercising regularly could ever be enjoyable. Fortunately, when it comes to food and exercise, you can find options that you actually enjoy. For example, if you dislike vegetables—broccoli in particular—then explore the vegetable world more carefully. Maybe you'd like broccoli if it were prepared differently, or maybe you can find a different kind of vegetable that tastes better to you. In any case, don't keep suffering through a food you can't stand.

The same is true for exercise. For instance, Mary S. loathed using gym equipment but found she enjoyed people watching along the bustling streets of Manhattan. She could walk from her apartment to Greenwich Village and back, logging four miles, and having a good time. Be equally inventive. Take the time to find the best of the worst. Keep experimenting until you find options that you actually enjoy. But by all means *don't commit to a plan you can't find a way to like*.

2. Tell the Whole Vivid Story. Ask yourself *why* you want to lose weight or improve your fitness. Most people spend too little time contemplating the answer. They give themselves generic or vague answers, like "I want to look better," "I want to fit into my clothes," or "I want to have more energy."

While these responses provide a starting point, they're too indistinct to carry you through moments of temptation—say a delicious piece of chocolate cake goes head to head with your "I want to feel good some-day" reason to avoid it. When a murky vision is all you have to conjure, the crystal-clear certainty of the cake will win every time.

Here's what John H. did to bring his vision into focus. He first described his motivation for losing weight and improving his fitness as "I want to look and feel better. I want to have more energy." This was not the whole story, nor was it vivid enough to keep his attention. So he went further.

3. Visit Your Default Future. Fortunately, when John looked at what might lie ahead for him, he was able to fill in the details. In his case, he made a mental visit to a rather prominent person who faced similar physical challenges.

"I thought of Larry M.," John explains. "He was a prominent local businessman, philanthropist, and family man. He was about my age and was also overweight like me. We even had the same body type. For the last several years I watched him suffer through diabetes, a heart attack, and kidney failure. He lost both his legs to diabetes, and then he died—still in his early sixties. Larry's unfortunate demise was my default future. So now, when I'm ready to order a T-bone steak, I focus on Larry M. I can see him right in front of me. Then I order the salmon instead."

Creating a vivid and believable image of your default future provides the detail you can draw on during moments of temptation. But it has to be specific and vivid. As John dug deeper into his reasons for changing, he was able to provide the detail he needed. That's key.

4. Use Value Words. After visiting your default future, distill some of your motivating insights into a Personal Motivation Statement you can use at crucial moments. Be sure to capture the feeling as well as the facts: "I'm doing this for my wife, Louise. It's the most heartfelt thing I can do to show her my love. It's like pearls and earrings times a thousand."

Notice the words John uses in his Personal Motivation Statement when describing what he's doing. These words shift John's emotions during these tempting times because they tap into his deeper values. They help John cast the temptation out of his head by helping him envision himself giving a precious gift to Louise, the woman he loves—"It's like pearls and earrings times a thousand."

By visiting his default future, telling the whole vivid story, and selecting value words, John was able to craft a statement that, if he meditates on it during crucial moments, can profoundly affect his emotions. To ratchet up the power, he combined this statement with a photo of Louise. The measure of a good Personal Motivation Statement is whether your use of it jars you out of the spell of temptation. If it doesn't, then it is too anemic. Keep at it until it reconnects you with what you really want when it matters most.

5. Connect to Who You're Becoming. Some people focus their Personal Motivation Statement on the person they want to become. For example, think of someone or a group of people who do what you hate to do right now but who actually enjoy doing it. Then, instead of dismissing them as crazy, become one of them. See yourself as one of them. As you follow through on your vital behaviors, pause and mentally celebrate the fact that you're becoming one of them.

For example, if you have trouble forcing yourself to work out, tell yourself (out loud!), "I'm an athlete in training, and this is what athletes do." Make this identity even more specific. Say, "I'm a hiker," "I'm a runner," or "I'm a skier"; then dig into this new interest more deeply. Read a hiking, running, or skiing magazine and imagine yourself in the pictures. Take your eyes off the sacrifice and place them on the accomplishment. Whenever you're tempted to revert to your old self, dispute the rationalizing thoughts with statements that tie you to who you are becoming.

6. Make It a Game. To finish off his motivation plan, John turned it into a game. He bought a device that displayed his calorie burn rate on a wristwatch. At first John tracked his burn rate; then he manipulated it. He learned that if he got up from his chair at work and walked up and down a few flights of stairs, not only did his burn rate double during the walk, but it took a full two hours to return to his sitting rate. Within two weeks John was posting his scores and celebrating his caloric consumption like an Olympic result. The behaviors themselves became more enjoyable because they were part of his achievement.

SOURCE 2: DO WHAT YOU CAN'T

1. Start with a Skill Scan. How many of the following are you readily familiar with?

- The numbers of calories in different foods—maybe not the exact numbers, but a rough estimate
- Alternative lower-calorie options you can substitute for the foods you're eating now
- Tasty recipes to prepare healthier foods at home
- How to use the labels on prepared foods at the grocery store
- Quick substitutions a chef can make to reduce the calories in your favorite dishes
- The pace to exercise at in order to burn the most fat
- The steps to take to stop a stitch in your side from hurting
- The best way to warm up before working out
- The optimal weight and repetitions to use when building muscle strength
- The minutes needed to burn fat and improve cardiovascular health

Of course, this list could have been far longer, and you don't need to know all the material in order to get started. To find the answers, begin with books, websites, or groups that are well established and offer mainstream advice, not quick fixes. Here are three websites that can get you started:

- www.nhs.uk/Livewell: This NHS-run website offers advice and information about healthy living, food and diet and weight loss.
- www.nutrition.org.uk: This is the website for the British Nutrition Foundation. It provides nutrition information for teachers, health professionals, scientists and the general public.
- www.nutritionaustralia.org: Nutrition Australia is an independent member organization that aims to promote the health and well-being of all Australians. The website provides resources and fact sheets as well as recipes.

For local information, check with your doctor's surgery or with a local hospital. Often they will have free outreach programs on weight loss, fitness, and wellness.

Of course, fitness and dieting skills may not be all you'll need to change your life. It may well be that your eating habits are tied to emotional issues you need to learn to address in better ways. As you study your crucial moments and ponder what keeps you from changing, scan for new skills you need to acquire, and include them in your plan. For example, if eating is tied to loneliness, you may decide to take a networking class at work as a way of developing new social skills.

2. Employ Deliberate Practice. Suppose you have a problem with snacking in the late evenings after dinner. For you, these hours have become a crucial moment. You can master this time period using deliberate practice. Here are the steps to follow:

- *Break the skills into bite-sized chunks and practice each skill in short intervals.* For example, take the time that includes dinner until bed, and break it into half-hour chunks. Then within each half hour, experiment with different eating, activity, and distraction options to figure out how to beat the strongest temptation within each half hour.
- *Get immediate feedback against a clear standard and evaluate your progress.* For example, once you've created a calendar that shows each evening in half-hour units and set some goals within those time frames (for example, twenty minutes of exercise and no more than a hundred-calorie snack), evaluate your progress each evening.
- *Prepare for setbacks.* Use your setbacks to adjust your plan. Maybe you went to a movie and ended up buying buttered popcorn or candy. Adjust your plan. Maybe next time you'll eat an apple on the way to the theater.

3. Learn the Will Skill. Many people believe that fitness and exercise are all about willpower—whether you have it or not. Will is important, but people forget that willpower is a skill with its own rules and tricks to practice.

For example, recent research shows that if people can *distract* their attention for just a few minutes, they can suppress negative urges and make better decisions.[8] Sharman W. used this idea to help her avoid cheating on her diet. She listed the ten reasons she wanted to lose weight and created the following rule: She could cheat on her diet, but only after reading her list and calling her sister. This extra step introduced a delay and brought in social support from her sister.

Other strategies our Changers use include taking short walks, repeating poems they have memorized, and drinking a glass of water. The key is to be aware of the impulse and to focus on something different until the impulse goes away.

SOURCES 3 AND 4: TURN ACCOMPLICES INTO FRIENDS

When it comes to personal fitness, here are two tactics Changers employ as a means of making the best use of social forces.

1. Add New Friends. Research in the Change Anything Labs shows that adding friends to your cause can improve your chances of success by as much as 40 percent.[9] *This is especially true for weight loss and fitness.*

For example, professor of medicine Abby King conducted an experiment with 218 people who were struggling to get enough exercise. All were encouraged to commit to walking at least thirty minutes a day. After the orientation, one group received phone calls every three weeks from a live person asking how they were doing with their goal and congratulating them for any success they had. This simple periodic nudge from a complete stranger resulted in a 78 percent increase in exercise (significantly more than those receiving similar reminders from a computer). The calls continued for a year—but even after the calls stopped, the new habits continued.[10]

Find a coach who can both motivate and instruct you. For instance, John H. actually hired a coach at his gym to supervise his workouts for his first month. They'd meet at six thirty a.m. three times a week. The appointment itself guaranteed that John H. would be out of bed and at the gym. He didn't want to waste his money or disappoint his coach. And his coach was able to show him the best way to use the different fitness machines and weights and how to build up his fitness without creating excessive soreness or injury.

Another kind of friend that's especially important is a *partner in training*—someone to diet or exercise with. This could be your life partner, a family member, or someone new. One of our Changers worked out with his brother, even though he lived in Seattle and his brother lived in Los Angeles. They followed the same exercise routine and texted each other every morning at six. The feeling of community and accountability that gave him was a huge source of motivation to get out of bed and to stick with his commitment. Having at least one other person who is on your same weight-loss and fitness program will do wonders for you both.

2. Hold a Transformation Conversation. There is one accomplice who absolutely must become your friend. It's the person who is your "nutritional gatekeeper." This is the person who does most of the food shopping, cooking, or other eating choices in your home. Of course, it might be you, in which case you're already in control. But if it's not you, or if you share this role, then you need to make your nutritional gatekeeper your weight-loss ally.

In some cases this person is just waiting for permission to help. Unfortunately, weight loss and fitness are sensitive topics, and people will usually wait for an invitation before stepping in. That means you'll have to make the first move. Ask the people who routinely influence your food and exercise decisions for their help. Explain what they can start doing to help you—for example: "Please buy more fruits to keep out and available." Share what they can stop doing—for example: "Please stop baking such delicious and tempting cookies or placing treats in highly accessible areas."

Finally, don't forget to let them know what to continue doing—for example: "I really enjoy and benefit from our evening walks together."

Don't limit transforming discussions to your nutritional gatekeeper. Most of the accomplices in your life would be shocked to discover they are hurting rather than helping you. They will welcome the chance to join in on your side. For more tips on how to hold this crucial conversation, go to ChangeAnything.com/exclusive.

SOURCE 5: INVERT THE ECONOMY

The existing economy often works against our fitness goals. As we suggested earlier, many packaged foods (especially items full of fats and sugars) have dropped in price, while prices of fruits and vegetables have gone up. Plus, you can get real deals if you supersize your purchases—leading to large purchases and servings. Many people believe that throwing away food left on their plate is criminally wasteful. These are just a few of the ways that outside incentives encourage us to eat and grow heavy. It's time to invert this.

1. Use Both Incentives and Loss Aversion. The good news about incentives is that they work. But there are conditions. Your weight-loss goals need to be short-term, one pound a week, for example, not four pounds a month. You need to take the system seriously—no cheating. And the rewards need to matter to you. Changer Deb W. created a star chart. Every time she lost a pound, she put a star on her chart. Whenever she got ten stars up, she shopped for new clothes—and threw away her old ones. Notice how the incentives worked. She got the new clothes she wanted and locked herself into her new size by throwing away the old ones.

2. Use Incentives in Moderation and in Combination. The best incentives are actually fairly moderate in size, and they work in combination with our own personal and social motivations.

Here is an example incentive plan one of the authors used. David wanted to lose twenty pounds in twenty weeks and bet two hundred dollars on himself. He gave the cash to a friend for safekeeping and set a weekly goal. David began at two hundred pounds, and his target weight was supposed to drop by one pound every week. Each Friday David would stand on his scale and take a photo to document his weight. He sent this photo to his friend Joseph because he believed Joseph would hold him accountable.

Any week that David missed his target cost him ten dollars, his self-respect, and the ribbing of his colleague. This simple incentive, when combined with all six sources of influence, worked. David lost twenty pounds and has kept the weight off for two years now.

SOURCE 6: CONTROL YOUR SPACE

1. Build Fences. Create barriers that keep bad stuff out and good stuff in. For example, once our Changer Mary S. realized she was the nutritional gatekeeper for her family, she tended the gate carefully. In fact, she conducted a food audit that looked like a search-and-destroy mission. Mary went through her refrigerator, cupboards, and pantry and around the apartment, removing junk food. She gathered up ice cream, candies, frozen pot pies, whole milk, chips, cookies, and even the cookie jar and gave them to a neighbor. She admitted that some of the items she gave away, like a perfectly good package of bacon, hurt her penny-pinching pride. But her motto became "We don't have to eat our mistakes!" Within thirty minutes her apartment was a safer place to eat.

Next, Mary made a shopping list of healthy alternatives to keep around the house. She put a fruit bowl on the table and kept it full. She also vowed to shop the outside edges of the grocery store and to avoid the aisles as much as possible. (The aisles are where the fat-filled engineered foods are kept. The perimeter is where fresh foods are stocked.)

Mary also put a mental fence across the middle of every restaurant menu. She discovered that appetizers and alcoholic drinks are the most calorie-dense items on a typical menu, so she also made the decision to stop ordering appetizers and alcohol in restaurants.

2. Manage Distance. John H. used distance to improve his fitness. He made exercising closer and more convenient. He purchased an extra pair of running shoes and a change of clothes and kept them at his place of work so he could work out right after work. He also bought a set of dumbbells and an exercise band and kept them by his desk. At home, John moved a TV into a spare room so he could work out while watching his favorite shows. Together, these little changes nearly doubled the time he spent being active each day.

3. Use Cues. We live most of our lives eating without noticing what or how much we're eating, and we also fail to see opportunities to add in a bit of fitness. Well-crafted cues can jolt us out of our routine and remind us of the options we have. A good one will catch your attention but won't embarrass you if others notice it too. It could be a personal saying like "Nothing tastes as good as healthy feels." It could be a photo of you being active or of a loved one who inspires you to be healthy. Often these cues not only remind you to eat right or exercise—they rekindle your personal motivation to do the right thing.

Remember, these cues should be placed so that they'll remind you during your crucial moments. If you tend to snack, then put some reminders on your fridge and cupboards. If your routine is to eat while you watch TV, then put a cue on the remote.

4. Use Tools. You can now find a whole host of high-tech tools that can help you eat right and exercise. ChangeAnything.com is a tool that can help in your effort to gain control of your fitness. Here are a few more examples of the kinds of tools that are hitting the marketplace:

- Accelerometers, pedometers, and even GPS systems you can use to measure and track your fitness
- Smart-phone apps for tracking your calories
- Armbands that track your calorie burn rate

Here are a few examples of simple, low-tech, but powerful tools.

- A paper calendar hung in the bathroom to chart your weight
- Smaller pans, serving bowls, utensils, and plates to help you reduce your portions
- A book of trail maps to help you explore your world

These are just a few of the things you can do to control your space. You'll need to find and use your own methods. You have to, because if you don't, you'll be surrendering to all the other people out there who are trying to control it for you.

Financial Fitness
How to Get—and
Live—Out of Debt

Financial fitness can be surprisingly hard to measure, track, or even understand. For instance, for forty years you think you're doing just fine with your retirement plan. How could you go wrong? You meet with your adviser, set aside the money...yada, yada, yada.

Then one day you graciously accept your gold watch and settle into your Barcalounger to watch *Law and Order* reruns whenever you darn well please, only to learn that you didn't set aside nearly enough money to survive your golden years. Actually, you do have enough money, as long as you don't buy anything. Or go anywhere. Or eat too often.

Or perhaps you're one of the lucky ones. You've retired and *do* get to buy things—but only when given permission by one of your children, who now support you. Like tens of thousands of other new retirees,[1] you're now living the life captured on the popular T-shirts people used to wear back in the eighties—the ones that said that the best way to exact revenge on your children is to live long enough to be a burden to them. Well, you've become a burden all right, but as it turns out, being a burden on your children may be funny on a T-shirt, but in real life it's a Greek tragedy.

Or how about this? No matter how fiscally responsible you are, financial stability is never in your control anyway. You pinch every penny until you accumulate a veritable fortune, and then the market falls and you're clipping coupons, not for recreation, but for survival.

So what's a person to do? One thing is for certain; it's a bad idea to take cues from your neighbors—unless, of course, you live next to a skinflint. But who wants to stockpile a mountain of cash while never buying so much as a new pair of socks? What kind of life is that?

Then again, you don't want to follow in the footsteps of your other neighbors either. It turns out that about 43 percent of American families spend more than they earn each year,[2] and they now have eighteen thousand dollars in high-interest debt.[3] They also have something like seventeen cents set aside for a financial emergency.

And yet they still buy things on credit—discretionary items that they've rationalized into calling "necessities" that their own parents would never have dreamed of owning without ponying up cold, hard cash.

"Not to worry," your neighbors exclaim, because as near as they can tell, "everyone is doing it." Besides, no matter their money woes, your financially stretched friends *do* find a way to scrape by every month. Of course, they're one medical emergency or even a parking ticket away from losing it all.

Are you similarly at risk? Could one missed paycheck start you on a downward spiral that leads to financial disaster? If four or more of the following statements apply to you, you probably are at risk in the short run and most assuredly are at risk come retirement time:[4]

- You owe more than seven creditors.
- You're a compulsive shopper.
- You and your life partner have lied to each other in the past six months about your purchases.
- You treat credit as cash, not debt.
- You frequently borrow to pay monthly bills.
- You see overdraft charges or late fees as a normal occurrence.
- You cover even small setbacks (home or car repairs, minor medical needs) with debt.

THE LIGHT AT THE END OF THE TUNNEL

Of course, not everyone is living a financial nightmare. Lots of people are financially fit—millions of them. And we even know how they got that way. They spend less than they earn. That magical act—simply spending less than you earn—lays the very foundation of financial stability: having a surplus.

The good news is that literally dozens of books teach how to manage that precious surplus. They teach what you should do someday in the distant, fuzzy future when you actually do have money building up in an account. If you've found a way to earn more than you spend, Armani-clad financial gurus will eagerly explain how to protect the excess, prepare you for the worst of circumstances, and secure your future.

But if you're like the vast majority of people around the world who don't have a surplus, a fat lot of good the investment and money management books will do you. Your challenge isn't ferreting out financial strategies to maximize the money that's piling up under your mattress. You have to find a way to change your current behavior so you'll accumulate a surplus in the first place. And that's what this chapter is about.

The following few pages will help you apply the Change Anything process to your own spending habits—which, according to popular financial adviser Dave Ramsey, is our real financial challenge in the first place. According to Ramsey, "Winning at money is 80 percent behavior and 20 percent head knowledge . . . Most of us know what to do, but we just don't do it."[5]

Here's what we do know. In order to become fiscally fit you can create a surplus by either earning more or spending less—or both. As you might guess, most people prefer earning more. In this chapter we'll look at what it takes to spend less. We'll help you develop a responsible plan you can live with, a plan that not only will help you develop new feelings and passions about financial habits but also will lead to happiness both today and in the future.

MEET SHIREE AND TYSON

To discover what it takes to create a financial surplus we'll seek the aid of two fiscally challenged Changers—Shiree and Tyson M. This lovely (and quite typical) couple first suffered from, and then resolved, serious financial challenges.

Shiree fell in love with Tyson when a bouquet of one hundred Mylar balloons arrived in the middle of story time with her twenty-seven kindergarteners. Her face flushed with happy embarrassment at being doted on so publicly. Then she had a fleeting thought that, on Tyson's graduate-student budget, this was a pretty extravagant expression after only one date. But she brushed her judgment aside in favor of the warm thought that Tyson was everything she wasn't.

Shiree had been raised by a banker whose "wallet squeaked when he opened it." While she loved clothes shopping, she felt pangs of guilt when she didn't get her pricey designer clothes on sale. So it seemed like a dangerous thrill to her when Tyson helped her into a helicopter on their first date and took her on a stunning flight up the Hudson River. He handed over his credit card for the five-hundred-dollar ride without taking his eyes off her.

Ten years into their marriage, Shiree worries that Tyson is bankrupting her. She does her best to rein in his outlandish spending and then resents him all the more when she has to feel guilty about a well-earned shopping spree. Their debt is mounting, their spending continues, and if something doesn't change soon, they'll lose it all.

IDENTIFY YOUR CRUCIAL MOMENTS

As you now know, the Change Anything process begins by identifying your crucial moments. So you'll need to give some thought to the moments that lead you into spending temptation. What are the characteristics of the times, feelings, or circumstances that lead to your financial missteps?

Tyson noticed that his spending was largely emotional. For example, it's a Saturday afternoon and he's bored and out of sorts. He's watching a ball game with an electronic accomplice sitting nearby, and in a half-alert state he whips out his laptop and begins surfing his favorite websites. In no time he has cornered his quarry—a new fishing reel. With a single click he finalizes his purchase, which produces a small thrill, followed by an empty feeling of disappointment. Staring at his computer screen, Tyson suddenly realizes that he has to change how he acts during these crucial moments of boredom or dissatisfaction.

For many consumers, their crucial moments have social roots. The Joneses entice them into buying things they don't need and didn't want—until *the Joneses* bought them, of course. Shiree's source of social influence lived with her. It kicked in every time Tyson violated some spending agreement the two of them had made. On bad days she would rationalize that if she blew the budget as well, perhaps he would begin to take some responsibility for their financial perils. Her counterintuitive plan never worked, but she kept doing it anyway.

Of course, the physical world can also stimulate irresponsible spending. Often Shiree would leave a store with two or three times more in purchases than she had planned. According to Paco Underhill, a well-known expert on consumer behavior, it isn't just high-end stores that break us down: Even supermarkets "are places of high impulse buying. Fully 60 to 70 percent of purchases there are unplanned."[6]

CREATE VITAL BEHAVIORS

Tyson and Shiree quickly realized that although it was true that they were far too spontaneous and out of control, they didn't *spend* every minute of every day. In fact, there were only a few crucial moments that they needed to watch for, and then they needed to act differently. After looking at their weak moments, they came up with their first, best guess as to what they should do. These initial vital behaviors would provide the starting point of their change plan. Later, when they faltered, they'd turn the bad day into good data by seeing if there was a new crucial moment they'd have to plan for—and a new vital behavior to help them master it. But initially, the four vital behaviors they chose were:

Track Everything. They would increase their awareness of their spending by recording everything in a mobile phone app.

Know Before You Go. They would make a precise list of what they intended to buy before they went to a store—and buy only items from the list.

Save Before You Spend. They would take 10 percent off the top of their paychecks to accelerate debt repayment.

Hold a Weekly Wealth Review. Every Sunday morning they would review what they spent, discuss deviations, and agree on the next week's budget.

ENGAGE ALL SIX SOURCES OF INFLUENCE

Of course, as Dave Ramsey said earlier, it's one thing to watch your crucial moments and identify what you should do to survive them; it's another thing to get yourself to *do* it. Here's how Tyson and Shiree used all six sources of influence to support their four vital behaviors.

SOURCE 1: LOVE WHAT YOU HATE

Visit Your Default Future. When they were truthful with themselves, Shiree and Tyson acknowledged that there was a lot about their financial situation they didn't like. Paying the bills invariably led to a heated argument. Then they'd clam up for weeks on end. The silent treatment not only hurt their relationship, but also kept them from examining their default future.

But how could they tap into their own best desires to change? How could they take a good look at what lay ahead for them if they didn't change? One of the turning points for Shiree and Tyson was a simple conversation they had one evening. What they did is remarkably similar to the powerful process of *motivational interviewing*[7] that anyone can use to help clarify their default future and connect to their most powerful reasons for change. Decades of research show that spending a small amount of time on this process produces substantial dividends in future change.

Here's how it worked. One night Shiree and Tyson decided to talk very explicitly about their reasons for changing. Initially they did so because Shiree was worried they didn't share a mutual purpose for their financial future. Specifically, she wasn't sure Tyson really saw the need to change his spending habits. She was afraid he was agreeing just to appease her and wouldn't follow through when she wasn't around. In retrospect, Tyson admits that Shiree's concerns were valid. He knew their finances were a mess, but he hadn't really paid attention to them.

So, Tyson and Shiree set aside an hour to interview each other. They would create a safe setting where the two could take an honest look at their financial life, their default future, and their personal motivations. The result would be a Personal Motivation Statement that would remind them of what they really wanted when the going got tough.

First Tyson interviewed Shiree. He took notes on her answers to a few crucial questions:

1. Where do you want us to be in ten years?
2. Where will we be in ten years if nothing changes?
3. What are the advantages of changing?
4. What do you intend to do?

At one point in the interview, both Shiree and Tyson broke down in tears. She had just asked Tyson where he would be in ten years if nothing changed. He looked stoic for a full minute, at which point Shiree began to think his mind had drifted. In irritation she said, "Sorry, is this topic too *boring* for you?" Tyson turned back to face her with moist eyes and said, "No, it's too *horrible*. I know that if I don't change I will lose you. And that would kill me."

When the two finished their interviews, they pulled some key quotes from their notes to create a Personal Motivation Statement that would guide their efforts. It included:

- We don't want to ever have another fight about money.
- Buying things has not made us happier; it's made us depressed.
- We will value peace more than pleasure.
- Getting something new is not worth losing our marriage.

Finally, after returning from their visit to their default future, the two made a promise that they would read their Personal Motivation

Statement each time they were tempted to violate one of their vital behaviors.

Tell the Whole Vivid Story. Tyson and Shiree changed their feelings about their choices by changing their story about their circumstances. In truth, they had previously never stopped to think about the big picture of their current situation. So, by using a variety of financial tools and techniques, they were able to get a more complete look at what their future held.

First they used a web tool to track all of their income and spending for thirty days. It took some work to track their earnings and spending, but once they did, it hit them like a blow to the stomach. They were currently spending about 10 percent more than they earned every month. If they continued to make their current payments on their credit cards, they would pay $18,371 in interest over ten years.

In addition to helping them feel differently about their bad habits, visiting their default future gave them hope for what lay ahead. The constrictions of a budget started feeling like a protective fortress that would keep them safe.

Make It a Game. To transform their budget from a pair of handcuffs to a helpful tool, Tyson and Shiree set goals and dates for their achievement. Shiree delighted in the idea of saving money. Putting money in an emergency fund was exciting. Each new deposit felt like a touchdown.

Even Tyson began to get into the spirit of the process when they turned it into a game. They created time-bound goals, aimed at small wins, and created a visible scoreboard. The first scoreboard consisted of a photocopy of each of their six credit cards. Then, underneath each card they wrote a date by which they could pay it off if they stuck with their plan.

Despite the fact that turning their plan into a game seemed a bit contrived at first, Tyson proudly admits that when Shiree handed him a black marker to give him the honor of crossing the first paid-off credit card off of their scoreboard, it felt like he had regained his soul. The second, third, and fourth milestones became increasingly motivating and often led to them feeling closer to each other than they had felt in a long time.

SOURCE 2: DO WHAT YOU CAN'T

When Shiree and Tyson conducted a financial *skill scan*, they quickly realized that they had all the wrong skills. They knew how to shop credit card rates, screen calls to avoid creditors, and avoid talking about their real future—to name but a few of their dodging techniques.

What they didn't have were the skills required for living in financial peace. They were ignorant about basic investment management. They were clumsy about tracking their financial status or assessing the impact of decisions they made. They never felt inadequate, because everyone they knew was equally unskilled. Most college students get an F (scoring 53 percent correct) on tests of basic financial literacy.[8] Our indebted couple was no different.

So the two set a course to become financially savvy. First, they became regular listeners to a radio talk show on personal finances. Next, they bought and studied a couple of highly recommended books. Then they discovered a free personal finance web application that made it easy to track their progress. Shiree loved knowing where their money was going and where their finances stood. Always the banker's daughter, she fell in love with her computer tools and the power they gave her to control her money.

Then, to deal with their biggest challenge, they worked on their *will skill*, or impulse control.

"We were far too spontaneous," Tyson explains. "At the supermarket checkout stand I'd throw in two breath mints, a magazine—and if it had been possible, a Lexus."

Their first line of defense against unplanned purchases was their vital behavior "Know before you go." By writing that precise list in advance, they didn't have to decide what to do each time they stumbled into a tempting new product. If it wasn't on the list, their answer was no. End of discussion.

Later, when they gained more control over their spending, they added a delay-and-distance tactic. In areas where they had some flex room, when they came across something they thought they might want and it fit in their budget, they'd write it down, return home, and then revisit the purchase twenty-four hours later. If they still thought it was okay, then they'd make the purchase.

SOURCES 3 AND 4: TURN ACCOMPLICES INTO FRIENDS

When it comes to shopping, many of the people you associate with are accomplices. Research shows that consumers have a much stronger impulsive urge to buy when they are shopping with others.[9]

Be careful about the negative influences of peer pressure. Remember what happened to our ten-year-old shoppers when we surrounded them with others who were snapping up horribly overpriced candy? Within seconds they were swept up in the social spending frenzy.

Here's what you can do to reverse this well-documented and powerful effect.

Redefine "Normal." One of the best methods to get social influence on your side is to get *yourself* on your side. Stop judging your self-worth by your net worth. Embrace the idea that happiness doesn't go to the person with the most toys. Take heart in the fact that there is no correlation between spending and happiness. There is a mound of research that suggests that a little exercise can bring you more pleasure than a thirty-thousand-dollar raise.[10]

The wonderful thing about redefining "normal" for yourself is that in so doing you inoculate yourself against all kinds of unhealthy social pressure. When others are going golfing on the weekend and the greens fee is out of your price range, you can comfortably say, "I'm going to pass," and not make yourself miserable with self-conscious ruminating. Learn to embrace simplicity and authenticity. It's incredibly liberating!

Hold Transformation Conversations. For most of us, cutting ourselves off from friends and family members who encourage us to spend irresponsibly is overkill. A more reasonable choice is to transform our spending accomplices into our friends. That's what Shiree and Tyson did. Obviously, since day one they had been accomplices to each other. Their indulgence in impulsive spending condoned and even provoked that behavior in each other. Fortunately, their mental visits to their rather bleak future motivated them to have a series of transformation conversations—with each other. One discussion at a time, they transformed each other into friends, and each mutually committed to becoming financially fit... together. Then, at their planning and review meetings, they sincerely complimented each other's integrity and celebrated each dollar of debt paid off and each dollar added to savings.

Next they took on larger social circles. They had talks with family, friends, and co-workers about what they were trying to do and asked each for his or her support. They suggested less expensive family reunions and talked with their friends about the need to change the location of some common get-togethers. Instead of meeting at a mall and walking the hallways, where temptation lurked in every store window, they started walking the neighborhood. Then, as they walked, they started sharing cost-cutting advice, shopping deals, and free entertainment venues.

Add New Friends. To help connect themselves to others who were trying to become more financially responsible, Tyson and Shiree developed a virtual "friends" network made up of hundreds of others who listened to a personal finance radio talk show. Adding these distant friends had a much greater effect than they ever imagined. The comments of one particular caller stuck with them for months. It was an elderly woman who was filled with remorse because she and her husband were ill prepared for the life they were living now in their seventies. She told the host how difficult it was some weeks to choose between medicine and food. Shiree was hit particularly hard by the story because Tyson had a heart condition that required some fairly expensive medication. She was horrified to think that one day Tyson might skip a week of medication so they could fill their car with gas, for example. A woman they never actually met had a powerful influence on their perseverance with their plan.

SOURCE 5: INVERT THE ECONOMY

As Shiree and Tyson succeeded in their plan, the intrinsic rewards were tremendous. Feeling in control was its own reward. They also loved reporting their progress in a family blog. As family members came to understand how important their financial goals were to them, they began to give electronic high fives, which meant a great deal.

But they also added an extrinsic reward to the formula. Their plan was simple. For every week they stuck to their financial plan, they rewarded themselves with a cost-free Wednesday night date. Just the two of them would spend time having fun together. Both were amazed at how much they enjoyed these midweek dates and did their best to not jeopardize their time together.

Take note: This was a low-risk, cost-free reward. They didn't walk through the mall; they walked through the park. They didn't buy dinner out; they ate at home and had an inexpensive treat.

SOURCE 6: CONTROL YOUR SPACE

Some of the simplest and most powerful changes Shiree and Tyson made were structural in nature. They made easy changes in a few physical factors that, in turn, made a huge contribution to their success. With time they came to realize that when it comes to financial fitness, Source 6 can become a powerful ally.

Use Tools. The most important physical device the two employed was a cell phone app that displayed how much they had left in each budget category. It even synced their combined spending so they could see the net effect of their actions. As simple as this application sounds, it had a profound effect. Like most bad habits, spending addictions are sustained by mindlessness. Their cell phone app helped them become conscious of the choices they were making while also helping them see their cumulative effect. By forcing them to make their choices mindfully, the simple, inexpensive app profoundly accelerated their change.

Engage Your Autopilot. Tyson and Shiree used their natural tendency to do nothing to their advantage as well. They set up an autopilot that made positive change the path of least resistance.

Their plan was based on very good social science. In the U.S. behavioral economist Richard Thaler created a retirement plan called Save More Tomorrow. Those who sign up for the program don't have to sacrifice today but instead agree to place some or all of their *next* salary increase into their retirement fund. They make this decision a year before the increase comes. Then when it actually arrives, they don't miss it because they've never adjusted to it. When people do this, they tend not to think about it anymore. They create the default setting and then let it control their destiny—in a positive direction.

That's exactly what Shiree did. She asked her HR department to automatically withdraw a modest amount from her paychecks for her retirement fund. But then she asked that 100 percent of her future salary increases be funneled in the same direction. Tyson made the same commitment with the retirement plan he had set up for himself. Three years into their automatic plans, Tyson is saving the maximum amount toward retirement and Shiree is also getting the full benefit of her company's matching contribution—all without torturing themselves over the decision over and over again.

Build Fences. Adults—just like the ten-year-olds we reported on in the first chapter—spend more carefully when they use cash. In contrast, credit cards, casino chips, and the like make it feel as if you were not spending your hard-earned money. It's funny money. So Shiree and Tyson built a "cash fence." That is, for six months they paid for everything in cash.

This decision turned out to be incredibly inconvenient but went a long way toward making the two big spenders fiscally aware. They began the experiment with some "plastic surgery"—they cut up all of their credit cards but one. In addition, they removed credit card information from all the websites where they were set up for automatic purchasing. Instead, if they made an online purchase, they would use a system to debit their checking account immediately. By making a one-time decision and then walling themselves off from these risky devices, they made their crucial moments far easier to handle.

Manage Distance. As we explained earlier, Shiree and Tyson avoided places that would tempt them to spend money. They turned down invitations to expensive restaurants or to pricey activities. Initially they limited themselves to grocery stores, and even then, they stuck to a sparse shopping list.

This distancing tactic was tough to begin with because the pair really enjoyed ogling and purchasing new merchandise. However, with time they learned to visit and enjoy new locales. For instance, their neighbor gave them an unused tandem bike, and after making a few alterations, they began taking an hour-long ride each evening. By placing themselves in interesting no-spend zones, they kept their distance from brick-and-mortar (as well as cyber-) dens of fiscal iniquity.

Change Cues. Tyson and Shiree did everything they could to remove buying cues from their environment. They also added cues that kept their attention on their long-term goals. They posted graphs showing their progress toward paying off their debts, they created a collage of the lifestyle (home, cars, and vacation) they'd like to enjoy guilt free someday. They even changed their home pages and favorites bookmarks on their computers to remove all buying cues.

Finally, in an effort to save money and the planet, they used a service to get their names removed from countless catalog mailing lists.[11] Over the course of the first year, their mail shrank by 90 percent. It took longer to get dropped from e-mail distributions, but through the magic of junk filters they even cleaned up their electronic cues fairly quickly. Again, they made these changes to get rid of the temptation of purchasing needlessly.

HOW ABOUT YOU?

Three years after embarking on an effort to change their financial situation, Tyson and Shiree have achieved remarkable results. They've paid off their car and credit cards, making them debt free except for their mortgage. With less money going to interest payments, they now make extra payments each month to pay off their condo in half the time (saving a fortune in interest).

Now that they have their spending under control—and budgeted in a way that creates excess rather than a deficit—Tyson and Shiree are adhering to the vital behaviors that financial gurus have been suggesting for years. They don't have (nor will they create) credit card debt, they stick to a monthly budget, and they set aside 10 percent of their income toward retirement.

As a result of their combined efforts, the transformed couple describe themselves as happy and relatively stress free. For the first time in their relationship, they now enjoy saving and feel optimistic about their financial future. Plus there's been an added bonus that came from solving their problem together. Both believe that their journey to fiscal fitness has strengthened their partnership.

Like those of others who are working to get out of debt, increase savings, and retire in style, theirs was not a straight line to success. They had some setbacks. Just like the rest of us, they had to learn and adjust. They know it's a continual process. But it is a known, tested, and effective process.

That means that you too can find ways to spend less and save more. You can overcome Dave Ramsey's observation that "most of us know what to do, but we just don't do it" by learning exactly how to do it. Decide what you really want, identify your crucial moments, create your vital behaviors, and then engage all six sources of influence. Do this and you can create that ever-elusive and wonderful thing known as a financial surplus. Do this and you can change anything.

Addiction
How to Take Back
Your Life

You don't have to be very old or particularly jaded to believe that once you're addicted to something (from gambling to crack cocaine), kicking the habit isn't going to be easy. Research shows that with certain dependencies, your brain can be altered for life—forever affecting your ability to feel pleasure—not to mention the fact that chronic drug abuse can harm both judgment and behavioral control, making it just that much more difficult to quit.

When you look up the word "addiction," it gets even more depressing. You read about *enslavement* and feelings of *euphoria* that, if interrupted, can lead to *trauma*, cravings, irritability, and depression. When you think about the hundreds of thousands of people who die from the effects of various addictions each year or if you listen to your aunt Sally talk about the hold nicotine has had on her since she first started smoking at age fourteen, you think to yourself, Can *anybody* actually kick an addiction?

But then there's the less publicized, more encouraging, side of the addiction literature. When you move from the headlines to academic journals, you learn that nearly all addicts recover. And the majority do it on their own.

An illustration of this rather startling good news unfolded in 1970 as the U.S. government waited for sixty-nine thousand heroin-addicted soldiers to return from the very site that got them addicted in the first place—Vietnam. Leaders worried that hospitals and jails would be overwhelmed by the problems associated with these addicted troops. But the problems never came. In fact, 88 percent of those who were diagnosed as "seriously addicted" kicked their habit shortly after leaving Vietnam.[1]

This remarkable transformation wasn't a one-off event. Scores of studies have shown that most people do, in fact, overcome their addictions, and many of them do so without any kind of therapeutic intervention. Now, why would this be? Why could tens of thousands of soldiers and even more citizens be able to successfully overcome enormous problems ranging from smoking to heroin addictions?

As you may have already guessed, many of the reasons lie in the first seven chapters of this book. The timeline for overcoming addiction is not set by a rehab center's calendar, genetic differences, or the underlying power of the addiction itself. Instead, the timeline is set by the speed with which individuals align all six sources of influence to help them change their habits.

Consider the sixty-nine thousand heroin-addicted soldiers who returned from Vietnam. The very action of returning home completely upended the six sources of influence that were supporting their current drug habit. After soldiers traded in their army boots for penny loafers, nobody was shooting at them, and their interests turned from land mines to matriculating, within months, almost all dropped one of the most addictive substances imaginable because all six of their sources of influence changed.

Contrast these returning soldiers with people who return from your typical high-end rehab site. After six weeks of counseling and separation from their drug of choice, patients return to their same homes, where they're now exposed to the same temptations, same accomplices, and same problems they had when they left—leading to the abysmal success rate of most rehab facilities.

The message from these examples should be both clear and encouraging. We're not suggesting that rehab has no value in helping people overcome addictions. For some, it plays an important role in helping them acquire skills. However, rehab shouldn't substitute for you becoming both scientist and subject as you develop your own six-source plan. Learn how to recruit power from everything from friends to the physical environment, and you can overcome any addiction.

BE PATIENT

Now, before we look into techniques for dealing with your particular addiction, let's start by examining what your habit has already done to you. That way, as a scientist working on yourself, you'll know what you're dealing with.

We'll start with your brain. As your addiction started gaining power over you, something subtle yet very profound took place deep inside your head. Many of the people you know don't understand what those changes have done to your brain, so they incorrectly accuse you of staying with your addiction simply because of the unholy pleasure it offers you. As far as the uninformed are concerned, you simply can't resist the high it gives you. In essence, *they* are caught in the willpower trap.

However, brain research reveals something you have felt even if you don't yet know it. With continued exposure to an addiction, sticking with your bad habit becomes less about seeking pleasure than about something else—something that began to reveal itself more than fifty years ago when two young scientists, James Olds and Peter Milner, started tinkering inside (of all places) rat brains. More specifically, Olds and Milner wanted to map the various functions of the brain—by location (something that was completely unknown at the time).

To uncover this invaluable information, the two researchers invented a process of inserting electrodes inside various regions of a rat's cranium and then pumping in a bit of electrical current. The experiment was mostly a bust. In most regions of the brain, the electricity produced no effect whatsoever.

But just when the two scientists were about to call it quits, they noticed that one rat behaved quite differently from the others. He seemed to *like* getting shocked. When given the option, he kept returning for more. Upon further inspection, the two scientists learned that this particular rat's electrodes had landed in a primitive part of the brain now known as the *septal region*.

Encouraged by the intriguing effect, the two scientists hooked electrodes to the septal regions of several rats and then set up a lever system whereby each could control the electrical shocks—*and* the accompanying bolt of joy. It wasn't long until the rats were pushing the lever incessantly. Many became so obsessed with the lever and the feeling it gave them that they pushed it until they collapsed from starvation and exhaustion.[2]

It's no surprise, then, that Olds and Milner concluded that these rats were having fun. Surely the rodents were stimulating themselves into a state of bliss. Dozens of brain researchers picked up on their finding, and it wasn't long until many saw the connection to human addictions. For decades, scientists assumed that addicts, like rats hooked to their precious levers, were driven by their lust for pleasure.

That is, until scholars began sticking electrodes inside human brains—and then doing something they couldn't do with rats. They asked those same humans what they were feeling. Now for the important finding. When human subjects explained how they felt when their "pleasure center" was being stimulated, they didn't use the word "pleasure" at all. They chose words like "urges," "cravings," and "compulsions."[3] This is an important distinction. When it comes to humans, the compulsive behavior Olds and Milner first observed in rats turns out to be related more to *wanting* than to *liking*. It's more like scratching an itch.

In one way, Olds and Milner got it right. Addictions as diverse as alcoholism, smoking, pornography, gambling, cocaine and heroin abuse, video gaming, shopping, and overeating all involve the septal region. In another way, however, the two researchers were wrong. Over time the motivation to continue with an addiction often transforms from seeking pleasure to satisfying cravings. Worse still, with repeated use of an addictive substance or act, the septal region of an addict's brain changes in a way that reinforces and maintains the cravings—making the addictions less satisfying but more compelling.[4]

This urge-creating mechanism helps explain why nearly half of all smokers who've undergone surgery for early-stage lung cancer resume smoking within a year.[5] This is also why the average alcohol or drug abuser who tries to quit is back at it within four to thirty-two days—even though the abuser hates what it's doing to his or her life.[6] Addicts—even when given a life-threatening warning such as early-stage cancer—don't fall off the wagon merely because they're looking to create a good feeling; rather, they're trying to resist a profoundly disturbing urge that surges up from within the primitive parts of the brain.

Hopefully this short historical review helps put your change plans in perspective. Research reveals that you *can* kick your addiction and it may not require an expensive treatment center. It's also clear that you'll need to be patient. Changes require you to overcome powerful urges stimulated from deep within the brain, and this takes time. It will also take several tactics. You will eventually need to amass a combination of the six sources of influence to keep you away from your addiction. You'll need to do this while your brain recovers from the insidious adjustments it has already made.

But take hope. Delaying gratification won't always be hard. Research shows that over time, withdrawal symptoms *will subside*. Next month will be easier than this month. The month after that will be easier yet. A year from now—although you may still have some lingering urges— your urges may be accompanied by a whole new set of feelings.

As your urges lessen or even subside, you're likely to look at former temptations with wonder and disgust rather than longing and fascination. This is certainly the case with former smokers, who often can't even stand the smell of tobacco once they've kicked the habit. The same can happen with other vices. You can literally learn to hate what you formerly loved.

IDENTIFY YOUR CRUCIAL MOMENTS

Now, let's turn to your personal addiction and what you can do to overwhelm it. To do so, we'll follow one of our Changers, Lee W., who struggled to quit a two-pack-a-day smoking habit for more than ten years—three years in earnest. While Lee's journey took longer than you might want to take, his path provides clues about how to not merely end your addiction but do so much sooner than he did.

Lee first tried to quit smoking when he developed bronchitis after a cold. He stopped smoking without any nicotine replacement or help. He cruised along without a blip until about a week into his reformation, when he found himself in a bar, drinking with a friend who smoked. When his friend lit up, so did Lee. And then he kept on smoking. Within a few days Lee was back to his old habit. For a year Lee refused to try quitting again—simply because he was convinced that he regressed because of his lack of willpower rather than as the inevitable result of a poor plan. You may have drawn the same erroneous conclusion about your previous, but failed, attempts to quit.

Lee's problem was with his plan. First, he failed to identify crucial moments. He was motivated to quit by an isolated event (the bout with bronchitis) that quickly passed into history. Lee also failed to create a robust six-source plan, and then he was blindsided by temptation in a crucial moment. *Since Lee fell into the willpower trap by erroneously blaming his lack of personal integrity and self-control, he succumbed to discouragement.*

Then Lee's circumstances slowly changed. His maturing children began to ask why he smoked. Concerned about being a bad role model for them, he decided to get back to work—not initially on himself, but on his change plan.

Lee started by examining his own crucial moments. He realized that while he was very motivated to not smoke most hours of the day, there were a handful of times or circumstances when his urge was greater than he could withstand. Lee's crucial moments came after meals, during breaks at work, when he was with family or friends who were smoking, and when he was drinking alcohol.

As Lee worked on his change plan, he had a chance encounter with a friend that improved his plan in an important way. Lee was describing his crucial moments to his friend Tiffany, when she said, "It's nice that you're trying to change how you respond during those moments, but shouldn't you first do your best to prevent those moments entirely? Why not get a patch?"

Lee had always thought of a patch or nicotine gum as a sign of defeat, and he told Tiffany as much. Their conversation grew a bit heated, and at one point Lee told her with a dismissive tone that "patches are just a crutch." Tiffany smiled at him for a few seconds and then said, "Exactly. And what idiot would refuse a crutch when his leg was broken?"

Lee bought patches that afternoon.

There's a lesson to be learned here. Even before you start identifying your crucial moments, use whatever resources you can to minimize your danger points. Sudden withdrawal from drugs such as heroin, barbiturates, and long-term alcohol use can cause agonizing and even life-threatening reactions and should not be attempted without help.[7]

So, think about getting a crutch. When your own brain becomes your enemy, you qualify for a crutch as much as anyone hobbling on a fractured tibia. Involve a doctor who can recommend or prescribe one of the many drugs that reduce withdrawal symptoms.

With that said, let's be clear that overcoming withdrawal

symptoms is not the same as kicking the habit itself. In fact, withdrawal symptoms play a relatively minor role in maintaining addictions. Just as using a crutch won't heal your leg, using a patch or similar device simply puts you in a better position to begin building the habits that will change your life. As we'll see later with Lee, the heavy lifting won't be done with these short-term aids. Over the long haul, you'll need to identify your crucial moments, create vital behaviors, and engage every one of the six sources of influence on your side.

CREATE YOUR VITAL BEHAVIORS

The fastest route to creating your own vital behaviors is to start with three actions typically associated with defeating an addiction. From there you can look to your own crucial moments and then tailor your own vital behaviors.

1. Say No. Since all addictions will eventually be solved by not engaging in the bad habit, the first and most important vital behavior is to say no.

Suggesting that you need to resist temptation by saying no is simple enough to do, but actually resisting the temptation can seem impossible—for all the reasons we've just described. Nobody is going to be saying at this point, "At last, now I know what to do. I need to stop putting cigarettes in my mouth. What was I thinking?"

The power of nominating "say no" as the first and most important vital behavior comes with the six-source plan that will motivate and enable you to do so.

2. Engage in Incompatible Activities. This next high-leverage action isn't so obvious. It involves distraction. Psychologist and addiction expert Stanton Peele suggests that recovering addicts need to engage in a meaningful activity that is incompatible with their current addiction. Dropping an addiction leaves a chasm. It's essential that you fill that hole with an incompatible activity—something that will absorb your time and interest, carry you on to higher accomplishments, and make it difficult for you to give in to your cravings.[8]

We can't tell you exactly what your distraction technique should be, but we can learn from Mimi Silbert, the head of San Francisco's Delancey Street (a residential program designed to help convicted felons and drug addicts turn their lives around). Since Delancey Street sports a better than 90 percent success rate, when Mimi talks, we ought to listen.

"You've got to get addicts out of their head," Mimi suggests. "For most of their lives they've thought about one thing—their own wants and cravings. So we assign each new resident another person to watch over. As our residents learn to care for others, they fill the void of their former addiction."

So, avoid focusing on your own cravings by focusing on others' needs and challenges. For instance, Lee started a blog to describe his journey to recovery—and help others do the same. As the weeks passed, Lee had more than a hundred people following his story—many of whom joined him in kicking a bad habit of their own. Working on his daily blog entries began to occupy Lee's attention in a way that both distracted him from his cravings and reminded him of why he wanted to drop the habit in the first place.

This second vital behavior helps in another way. Recovering addicts often spend a considerable amount of time blaming themselves and being criticized by others, and their self-esteem suffers. However, when they help another person succeed, it can go a long way toward helping them earn back their self-respect.[9]

3. Become Physically Active. There is a third vital behavior for overcoming addictions, and although the science isn't completely settled yet, contemporary research into brain activity is so promising, we'd be foolish to overlook it.[10] The latest science suggests that as you start to lay out your personal plan, you should include physical activity. You can walk, run, swim, climb stairs—any form of aerobic exercise appears to help.

How does physical activity help with addictions? Think about the symptoms you feel when your cravings are really kicking in: nervousness, anxiety, sweaty palms, and an upset stomach. A quick-step walk around the block will often eliminate most of these symptoms. Plus physical activity seems to reprogram the brain's internal circuits, which, if left unchanged, would maintain addictions.[11]

ENGAGE ALL SIX SOURCES

SOURCE 1: LOVE WHAT YOU HATE

Lee admits that he enjoyed smoking a bit. He didn't love it, but then again he couldn't imagine *not* smoking. Plus, whenever he went more than two hours without a cigarette, he began to feel jumpy, distracted, anxious, and frazzled. He described going without cigarettes as "going crazy." How was he ever going to learn to love *that*?

Lee began by taking withdrawal symptoms seriously. Research

confirms that people who taper off of their addiction or use a replacement therapy are more likely to succeed in the end.[12] So Lee used patches and later nicotine replacement gum to help with his withdrawal symptoms. Of course, these were just a start. But they made it easier to stay personally motivated to change.

To add to his personal motivation, Lee thought about his long-term aspirations and the role smoking played in them. He *told the whole vivid story* of why he wanted to quit. He started by writing, "I want to quit so I can feel healthy, live active, and be here for my children and grandchildren." That statement was sort of a bland start, so he made it more graphic by adding a more vivid reminder of his default future.

Lee placed on his mobile phone a photograph that showed him holding his baby daughter. To most people the photo looked like nothing more than a tender memory of someone he loved. But to Lee the picture sparked feelings of determination because of the history behind it.

Here's the whole story. Shortly after Lee's wife snapped this picture, Lee lifted his smoldering cigarette to his mouth. Since it had taken a few minutes to pose and take the picture, the ash at the end of the cigarette had become long, so when the butt struck Lee's mouth, the ash dropped . . . onto his daughter's upturned face. And while Lee felt awful about dropping ash on his little girl, he felt even worse about how his habit was likely to affect her in more lasting ways. Lee saw the dropping ash as a symbol of everything she might suffer as she experienced the devastating and crippling effects of either second- or firsthand smoke.

So Lee popped the photo onto his phone and then added another sentence to his Personal Motivation Statement. "The Ugly Truth: When I choose the next cigarette, I'm putting cigarettes ahead of my daughter." This harsh, unflattering statement helped Lee tell the whole vivid story in crucial moments when he was tempted to light up one more time.

Next, to help change how he felt about these decisions, Lee made a commitment that before lighting up a cigarette, he would stare for thirty seconds at the photo on his mobile phone and read aloud his Personal Motivation Statement. If after doing this he still wanted to smoke, he could do so.

Lee also used *value words* to counter the excuses he sometimes told himself. Whenever he was tempted to say, "I'll have just one," he would challenge the thought by saying, "I will become a smelly smoker again." When he caught himself thinking, "I need a smoke," he'd verbally respond, "I'll never be a sucker again!" Lee found that making audible and explicit responses to these thoughts literally changed how he felt about his choices.

About a year into his struggle, Lee received a phone call from Raul, a former friend—actually, more of a former smoking buddy. When the company Lee worked for went smoke free, throwing him and the other smokers out into the back alley during their breaks, people who might not have ordinarily hung out together now did. Despite the fact that Raul was nearly twice Lee's age, they became buddies.

For three years, until Raul retired, the two talked about kicking the habit, but it was just talk. Neither made any progress. Raul was now calling to see if Lee knew the phone number of still another one of their alley smokers—and then the conversation turned to the latest goings-on. It turned out Raul was in the hospital recovering from lung surgery. It didn't look good. In a flash, Lee was thrust into what he felt just might be his default future. He thought of lying helplessly in a hospital bed every time he felt tempted to smoke.

Lee also focused on building a new Lee by exploring the opportunities that being a nonsmoker would create for him. He decided to add to his roles of father, husband, and provider a new role. He would also be a hiker. Lee's wife and daughters were thrilled with their new weekend treks. He had read that exercise was a good way to suppress the urge to smoke, and the article was right.[13] Lee never felt jumpy, fidgety, withdrawal feelings when he was striding up a hill.

One of the most important motivational tools Lee used was to take his overall strategy and *make it a game*. He stopped thinking of quitting as a lifelong quest and began breaking it into small wins. His first increments were only a day. And, as in any good game, he kept score. He created a chart that he posted privately in his closet. Each day he would place an *X* on the chart, demonstrating how many consecutive days he had "won." Then he would set his next goal—another single day. Thinking of daily challenges rather than lifetime struggles gave him a sense of hope and determination that increased his motivation substantially.

As Lee created intentional tactics to help him feel more motivated to change, his feelings about his cravings transformed. He began to feel pride and satisfaction when he went another week without relapse. *Quitting became pleasurable rather than painful.*

SOURCE 2: DO WHAT YOU CAN'T

When Lee conducted a *skill scan*—examining both his abilities and his knowledge—he realized that he didn't know much about addictions. So he read a couple of popular books, checked out some websites, and talked to his doctor. Lee was surprised by what he uncovered. For instance, he'd thought that once he was past the withdrawal symptoms, he'd be done with smoking. Now he understood that urges, on some level, were likely to continue long after his withdrawal symptoms ended. He wouldn't let that catch him by surprise.

Lee also learned that depression is quite prevalent among smokers and addicts of all stripes—even kids who are addicted to video games.[14] Furthermore, this depression is a major barrier to recovery.[15] Lee didn't think of himself as being depressed, but he talked to his wife about it and they decided to check in with each other every evening to review each other's days and to "count their blessings."

Most importantly, Lee took steps to *learn the will skill*. He knew he'd continually find himself in tempting situations, and he worked to develop strategies for dealing with each instance. Most of his strategies involved distraction techniques—for instance, Lee learned that his own urges have peaks and valleys and that the most powerful peaks lasted around twenty minutes. So Lee found activities that he could use to distract himself until the urge subsided. He already had added exercise to his antismoking quiver. He jumped rope, did jumping jacks, or merely jumped in place until his heart was racing and he was gasping for air. To further distract himself, if one of his family members was around, Lee would immerse himself in what they were doing. He'd help his older daughter with her homework or talk to his wife about her day.

A few months into quitting, Lee discovered he could actually use magic to reduce his urges. Part of a smoker's addiction is tactile. Lee longed to hold a cigarette in his hands and fingers. So he put this compulsion to use by learning close-up magic tricks. Lee kept cards and coins nearby and found he could often master a new trick in about twenty minutes of deliberate practice. Lee refused to fiddle with and eat food as a means of satisfying his tactile urges. He knew that eating was one of the most common distractions people use, and he didn't want to gain weight.

SOURCES 3 AND 4: TURN ACCOMPLICES INTO FRIENDS

Lee's wife had quit smoking when they started having children, and she clearly wanted him to quit as well. However, she didn't want to turn into a nag. Plus, Lee didn't want to be nagged. After a few failed attempts to talk about the issue, Lee's smoking had become a no-discussion zone. Whenever he lit up, she clammed up.

But this was just plain stupid. The two would have to find a way to talk honestly and respectfully. So Lee held a *transformation conversation*. He sat down with his wife, explained his plans, and then asked her for help. To avoid nagging, they agreed that it would be okay for her to celebrate any success she might observe him enjoying and to ask at the end of each day how well he had done.

Lee also had two conversations that *distanced him from the unwilling*. The first was with his father, an adamant smoker, who lived just blocks away. Lee didn't want his actions to offend his father. Lee explained that he needed to stay away when his father was smoking but wanted to stay close as a son. To his surprise, his father was supportive, saying his granddaughters deserved clean air.

Lee held a second distancing conversation with his smoking friends at his latest job. These were the folks he could beg a cigarette from anytime he needed one. Again, Lee was concerned that his quitting might offend a colleague or even end a friendship. And again, people were more understanding than he'd expected. Like most people, they didn't begrudge a person giving up a habit—particularly when it's widely seen as unhealthy.

Lee also *added new friends* by joining an outdoors club that organized weekend hikes. The club was made up of nearly all nonsmokers and introduced Lee and his family into a whole new circle of outdoor enthusiasts. In retrospect, Lee was surprised at how influential another group of friends was.

About a month into his change effort, Lee felt bold enough to put a declaration on his Facebook wall. He let his 213 "friends" know that he was quitting smoking and that he would report every day on his three vital behaviors. Eventually the report turned into a simple count of how many days of "healthy living" he had achieved. More than half of these friends would regularly give positive feedback on his page. Lee began to look forward to giving the nightly report and would secretly check his account at work because it felt so gratifying to see the accolades pour in.

SOURCE 5: INVERT THE ECONOMY

Lee told his daughters he was putting his money where his mouth was by *using carrots... and the threat of losing carrots*. Here's how Lee was able to invert his economy. He calculated he was spending about $5.50 a day on cigarettes, so he went to the bank, secured a stack of forty one-dollar bills, and put them in a display box in the living room. Then Lee told his girls, "This is the money, forty dollars a week, that we'll spend on family outings and other fun stuff—if I don't burn it up in cigarettes."

Then, every week on Friday the family would sit together and discuss how Lee had done. Lee was scrupulously honest about his lapses, demonstrating to his girls that honesty was more important than succeeding every time. If he had smoked on one of the days that week, then he would remove $5.50 for that day from the recreation fund. Then the family would plan their weekend adventure with the money that was left. Whenever Lee was about to light a cigarette, he would imagine how disappointed his girls would be, and it helped him resist temptation.

After a few months with more successes than setbacks, Lee and his wife decided to invest in their smoke-free future. They did this in a way that took advantage of *loss aversion*. The two of them took down their tobacco-scented curtains, had their carpets professionally cleaned, washed their walls, and threw out Lee's smoking chair. Then they brought in new curtains and a replacement chair. All of this would be wasted if Lee went back to smoking. For Lee, it felt as if he were scrubbing away his old life and revealing his new one.

SOURCE 6: CONTROL YOUR SPACE

Sometimes addicts leave their bad habits behind by making a whole-sale change in their environment. They enter an in-patient treatment center or move across the country. But you needn't be so dramatic to draw on the power of *things*. Sometimes small, simple changes in the physical world can be equally effective in turning one's environment into an ally.

For instance, Lee took immediate steps to *build fences* between himself and cigarettes. He and his family went on a "search-and-snuff" mission, scouring their home to find and get rid of cigarettes, ashtrays, lighters, and other smoking-related objects. Lee also went through his car and workplace to make sure they were all tobacco-free zones.

They also worked to *remove the cues* that used to prompt Lee to smoke. That was one of the reasons they replaced his smoking chair. He put up a sign next to his wet bar that stated: "Drinking ≠ Smoking." Lee also set decks of cards where ashtrays used to sit. The cards would be there to give him something to do with his hands.

Finally, Lee made use of *tools*. As we suggested earlier, Lee used his mobile phone and computer network to remind and encourage himself to change. Before each meal (when he knew he would have the time to smoke and would be tempted) Lee programmed his phone to bring up a photo of his children, people walking in the woods, a shot of a person lying in a hospital bed, and other reminders of what he wanted and didn't want in life.

HOW ABOUT YOU?

Tens of thousands of American soldiers dropped an aggressive and powerful heroin addiction by completely upending their world. They left the steamy jungles of Vietnam and kicked their addiction in a matter of weeks. That's what happens when you engage all six sources of influence at once.

Most people take a more circuitous route. Lee certainly did. Why? Because like most people, Lee discovered many of the strategies he used to succeed through a lengthy process of trial and error. Each time he had a setback, he didn't give up and become discouraged, but instead examined the new crucial moment and came up with tactics for dealing with it.

You now have access to a robust and engaging website— ChangeAnything.com. If you haven't checked it out yet, you should now. It's filled with six-source techniques and solutions, which means that, unlike Lee, you don't have to discover by yourself most of what you'll need to do. Instead, you can review your crucial moments, create your very own vital behaviors, and then put into play at least one tactic from each of the six sources of influence we've just reviewed. You can make and start this robust plan right now.

Don't Go It Alone. Take note. If your challenge is a substance addiction, then it's especially important to check in with your doctor first. Drinking and drugs can have bad health consequences that will need to be managed even as you quit your addiction. In general, confidentiality and doctor-patient privilege laws make it safe to involve your doctor, even when your addiction involves illegal substances. Even if your addiction is purely behavioral, doctors and clinicians may be able to provide you with tools that will help mitigate some of the negative symptoms as you get through the first few weeks or months.

Remember, You're the Rule, Not the Exception. As most people study what it takes to kick an addiction, they quickly decide that, unlike the people in the success stories we've shared, they won't have to go to so much work. Instead, they'll use their superhuman powers to resist temptation and choose merely one or two tactics from the material we just covered. That's right, a good talk with their best friend plus a few months of gutting it out and they'll do just fine. Once again the willpower trap claims another victim.

Don't kid yourself. You're a human being. That means you're not an exception to the rule that you need to overwhelm your problems by attacking them with all sources of influence. Remember, any sources you don't use to your advantage are likely to be working against you. And although putting together a more robust change plan may involve more tasks, over the long run it will result in a whole lot less struggle and failure.

In fact, if you take the time to continually study what works for you and what doesn't, then, if you make changes to your plan to suit your newly discovered challenges, you—along with your six sources of influence—can change anything.

Relationships
How to Change Us by Changing Me

This chapter is written to those who believe their relationship could be substantially improved if they changed their own (rather than their partner's) behavior. After all, this is a self-help, not a change-others, book.

If you're now thinking, "What? Changing myself isn't going to fix my relationship problems. I'm not the problem person in our relationship!" read on just a bit. Then decide whether this chapter is for you or not.

We know a lot of people will opt out of this chapter because, according to research at the Change Anything Labs, more than 90 percent of those in troubled relationships are convinced the primary cause of their problems is *their partner.* Since we're guessing some of our surveys were filled out by both partners in some relationships, we suspect this number ought to be held a bit suspect.

So before you decide this chapter isn't for you, please suspend disbelief for just a moment.

To capture your curiosity, we'll start by sharing information so intriguing in nature and so important to your relationships, you'll be eager to learn more. We're referring, of course, to the important findings in the field of colonoscopies. That's right, when it comes to your most important relationships, colonoscopy research has a great deal to offer.

This curious line of inquiry all started when Nobel laureate Daniel Kahneman asked patients who were being subjected to a colonoscopy to rate their level of discomfort during the course of the *unanesthetized* procedure. The results were rather surprising. It turned out that the comfort rating had almost nothing to do with the total amount of pain the subjects felt during the awkward and uncomfortable process! The only thing that mattered was how painful it was *at the end.* (Sorry.)

Kahneman describes the two colonoscopy studies. The first was naturalistic. He didn't control how long the colonoscopy took, but he asked people to rate their pain every sixty seconds. Interestingly, the duration of the procedure didn't predict the memory of pain. Instead, it was predicted by the maximum pain and the pain in the final few minutes.

During the second experiment, Kahneman had the physician leave the probe in without moving it for the last sixty seconds. This "recency manipulation" had a huge impact on the memory of pain.[1] When the procedure ended well, the subjects recalled the experience as far less unpleasant. It turns out that human beings judge much of their life experience (colonoscopies included) not on the totality, the average, or a glance back at the entire experience, but on the basis of the *last few minutes.*

So what does this have to do with your relationships? Everything. Much of what you're feeling about your daily relationships stems from only a few moments that overwhelmingly color your perception. For instance, when you ask people about the quality of their marriage, they rarely draw conclusions based on the overall experience. It could be that in the previous hundred hours together they enjoyed ninety-nine and a half hours of peace and warmth. However, if thirty minutes ago it went very poorly, people tend to describe their *entire relationship* from the *memory* of that half hour rather than the *experience* of the one hundred.

For example, consider work relationships. If your boss is reasonable, in control, even pleasant most of the time, but, say once every three months becomes very angry and verbally abusive— that seemingly random and always horrible experience colors everything else.

"But I haven't lost my temper in more than three months," the boss explains to a friend. "Why are people so nervous around me?" Because after one or two such outbursts, all other normal interactions feel strained—as the direct report waits for the boss to explode. Actions that occur less than 2 percent of the time affect the other 98 percent.

The same is true at home. Poignant negative experiences paint the entire relationship. When relationship scholars Lowell Krokoff and John Gottman interviewed couples to learn what led to relationship happiness, they learned that satisfied pairs routinely recount happy times—seeing good even in their struggles. In contrast, unhealthy couples interpret the past in a negative light—seeing even extended happy times as simply a long pause in their misery.[2]

IDENTIFY YOUR CRUCIAL MOMENTS

Why would some couples look back at their relationships and see everything through a negative lens while others recalled them fondly? If Kahneman is right, it's based at times on small, poignant, or recent experiences—but what kind of experiences?

When the well-known marriage scholar Howard Markman conducted studies into marital happiness, he was able to identify four specific actions that predict with 90 percent accuracy who will remain happy in their partnership and who will look back through lenses of regret and recrimination.

According to Markman, you need not count how many happy moments the couples have together—healthy and unhealthy relationships have about the same number. Instead, watch how couples argue. That's the key crucial moment to closely examine. More specifically, watch for what Markman refers to as "The Four Horsemen of the Apocalypse." These four highly predictive behaviors are criticism, defensiveness, contempt, and stonewalling.[3] Couples who routinely rely on these harmful tactics during an argument are very unlikely to remain happy in their relationship.

You'll note that the first three of Markman's horsemen could be considered forms of psychological violence and, quite frankly, seem to be rather obvious predictors of dissatisfaction. It's hard to attack one another and remain satisfied with a relationship. In contrast, the last horseman (stonewalling) is a form of silence and could easily be seen as less important. But that would be wrong. Silence is actually a powerful predictor of dissatisfaction. Related research shows that only 40 percent of divorces are caused by frequent and ferocious fights. Instead of going at it vociferously, couples learn to avoid skirmishes by avoiding each other. Over time, their friendship fades and the relationship withers.[4]

Our own experience with producing interpersonal problem-solving training has repeatedly taught us that interactions often go awry after a small, even trivial, change in behavior. When we direct actors in scenes that have been written to demonstrate how an interaction can turn from pleasant to abusive, we don't direct them to transform their smiles into screams or their suggestions into threats. Instead, a jaw tightens, an eyebrow raises, a lip curls—ever so slightly—and that makes all the difference. If you were to measure the deadly behavior changes in millimeters of facial movement, or foot-pounds of teeth grinding, or decibels of volume, the changes would be quite small. Nevertheless, the emotional impact can be profound.

Other small actions can have a large *positive* impact. For example, University of Utah psychology professor Timothy Smith recruited 150 couples with an average marriage tenure of thirty-six years. He asked these seasoned couples to discuss a topic they had a difficult time resolving. Many launched into stressful exchanges about chores or spending. None enjoyed the exchanges—who can blame them if they still hadn't figured them out after almost four decades of trying!

But some couples did little things the others didn't. Even as the talking heated up, there would be occasional expressions of warmth. At times it could just be a tiny term of endearment tacked onto the beginning of an expression of frustration: "Sweetheart, I can't understand a word you're saying!" With others it was just moving in a smidge closer or making contact foot to foot.[5]

Smith discovered not only that these little gestures profoundly related to happiness with the relationship, but also that their presence related to substantial decreases in heart disease as well. Talk about a vital behavior!

COULD *I* BE A KEY TO *US*?

Patricia S. began thinking about breaking up after watching three different friends go through divorces. Suddenly this option seemed viable. Patricia struggled to decide whether she was willing to let the challenges she had endured for two decades cloud her next twenty years as well.

She had not signed up to be the only person in the pair who seemed invested in the relationship—or even took the trouble to talk. Her husband, Jonathan's thoughtful aloofness seemed fascinating when they were dating, but over the years she saw it more as disinterest than depth.

Patricia also had not intended to be the parent who did most of the child rearing. She had planned on a partnership. She was also spending much more time on the job than she had originally intended when they elected to have children. But given Jonathan's somewhat meager income and apparent lack of drive, it was a matter of survival. With all Patricia was going through, it didn't take much nudging to make dissolution look like a reasonable solution. It appeared that the problem was *him*. Logically, then, getting rid of *him* would solve it.

But the increasingly obvious answer to her problems got more complicated one day after a fight with her teenage son. Patricia had become frustrated with her son because he had developed a habit of lying to her. After uncovering yet another deception, she laid into him about it. In the midst of her diatribe, he looked away and said softly, "Mum, I *have to* lie to you."

"What? What do you mean you *have to* lie to me?"

"Mum, you may not want to hear it, but both of us kids have learned that if we tell you the truth, you yell at us. So we hide it from you as long as we can."

Patricia couldn't breathe. While under other circumstances she might have become quite angry at this accusation, his gentle but blunt expression completed a picture in her mind that she could not ignore. She suddenly saw connections between people's reactions to her at work and at home—including the silence and distance of her husband. The *simple* story that attributed her dismal marriage to her husband's obvious issues began to appear *simplistic*—maybe even distorted.

That pivotal moment with her son started an episode of self-examination that opened up a new possibility for Patricia. She began to suspect that changes in her own behavior might substantially affect the relationship. True, her husband wasn't perfect, but then again, *she* was the person over whom she had most control. She could change herself. She was far from certain that changing herself would lead to an improved relationship, but she decided to give it a try.

BE THE SCIENTIST AND THE SUBJECT

To discover what's going wrong in your relationships, you'll need to explore your own successes and failures. Patricia started by searching for the crucial moments that led to the unhealthy conversations that were disrupting their entire relationship. Their number one problem was easy to spot: For twenty-three years, the two of them followed an unhealthy pattern. In Patricia's words, "At the end of the month, every month, we don't have enough money to pay the bills. I fume and complain to Jonathan, and he is unresponsive. Then I become upset and he gets up and walks out of the room."

This conversation took place a dozen times a year in a sadly similar way. It was a truly crucial moment for Patricia and Jonathan because the fallout of the predictable pattern affected their feelings toward each other for days and even weeks afterward. The bad behavior in this conversation had two triggers: money and Jonathan's silence.

Issues related to both of these topics created most of the crucial moments in their family because they poked at two of Patricia's violated expectations. First, she had never counted on being the driven career person of the pair. Second, her life plan didn't include a husband who rarely expressed affection, acted like a partner, or showed an interest in anything outside of his own world.

But then Patricia put on her scientist hat and looked for times when the financial-shortfall conversation or discussions about greater involvement in parenting the children *didn't* lead to a heated argument. She looked for the *positive deviance* in their marriage. Sometimes Patricia behaved slightly differently when she talked about their challenges, and the conversation went much better. Now, if she could only identify the specific tactics that worked and turn them into habits. After thinking about it for a couple of days and seeking advice from her best friend, Patricia identified the following three vital behaviors.

1. Think, "It's Not Wrong; It's Just Different." Patricia noted that when potentially stressful conversations went well, before opening her mouth, she would compare Jonathan to Jonathan rather than Jonathan to Patricia. Jonathan got things done—but he did it at his pace and in his way. Patricia discovered that when she stopped trying to make him a male version of herself, she felt differently and the conversation went more smoothly.

2. Shut Up. Patricia also learned that if she would allow periods of silence in the conversation, Jonathan would talk a lot more. She tended to fill every silence with a new verbal assault—especially about how frustratingly silent Jonathan was being. She found that when she shut up, it encouraged his participation.

3. Speak with Respectful Candor. Patricia noted that she often mistook combat for candor. She would share her concerns through aggressive out-bursts that she justified as simply being honest. So Patricia made an action rule for herself. When she was frustrated with Jonathan, she would learn to express her concerns in a respectful way.

Patricia concluded that if she could simply get herself to drop some of her judgments, practice silence, and share concerns more respect-fully, their conversations would go much differently. If these few crucial moments went differently, she surmised that their entire relationship could feel different.

ENGAGE ALL SIX SOURCES

Once Patricia articulated what she wanted to do—more specifically, the vital behaviors that she thought might turn her relationship around— then she had to find a way to both motivate and enable each of the behaviors. That, of course, is where the six sources of influence come into play.

SOURCE 1: LOVE WHAT YOU HATE

Tell the Whole Vivid Story

If you're like most human beings, the current story you tell about your relationship is predictable. You portray yourself as the innocent victim ("I have to do all the hard work!"), your partner as the malignant villain ("He never listens!"), and your circumstances as so vile and complicated as to make you trapped and helpless ("There's no use talking to him; nobody can get a word in edgewise!").

Unfortunately, if you tell your story in this manner, you're likely to feel smug, self-righteous, and justified in your actions as you lash out at the villain you call your partner. But that's no problem, because he or she deserves it. And, truth be told, your partner probably is also acting in all kinds of unhealthy ways. He or she is a human being, right?

Our point is not that your story is wrong; it's that it's incomplete. You're leaving your own behavior out of the spotlight, and you're the one you're most likely to be able to change. You need to tell the whole vivid story, including your partner's positive behaviors along with some of your own problematic ones.

He's Not a Villain. Patricia's feelings about her vital behaviors changed profoundly when she started to intentionally recall virtues Jonathan had displayed in the past. For example, not long before she started thinking about divorcing Jonathan, Patricia came down with a virulent virus that presents the host with some awful symptoms. When Patricia was feeling particularly frustrated with Jonathan, she would recall how he responded to her illness.

"He did everything for me. He left the house at two a.m. to get medication one night. When I repeatedly vomited and made an awful mess, I was so ashamed and apologized to him. He looked at me, surprised, and said, 'I love you. This is part of it.'

"In the moments when I would recall those experiences, I could not feel the same self-justified rage at him. It made it much easier for me to practice silence and speak more respectfully." In addition to recalling her husband's virtues, Patricia learned to stop framing issues of simple preference as fundamental differences in character. For instance, Patricia had believed that Jonathan's slowness to respond meant he was heartless and uncommitted—while her candor and energy in the argument demonstrated her commitment and loyalty. However, when Patricia began describing Jonathan's approach as thoughtful and deliberate, rather than uncommitted and heartless, her feelings changed profoundly.

I'm Not an Innocent Victim. Eventually Patricia changed her story from "I'm the one who has the courage and commitment to have the hard conversations" to "I can be too forceful at times." Making this change didn't mean that Patricia was taking all the blame. Jonathan did play a role in their problem. The change of story simply meant that she was taking responsibility for her role while letting Jonathan take his. And when she told the whole vivid story, she felt more inclined to attempt small changes in her behavior in hopes of seeing new responses from Jonathan as well.

And she did. As Patricia made it safer for Jonathan to enter the conversations, he opened up. She began to discover that he cared immensely about the relationship and became more tolerant of his different approach to their interactions—no longer seeing it as "It's either my way . . . or the *wrong* way."

Visit Your Default Future

Patricia's default future was clear to her. If she didn't find a way to bring about changes in how she (and they) interacted, she would continue to feel isolated and resentful, while establishing a tense and possibly harmful atmosphere for the children. She could change all that with a divorce—and then experience both the pros and cons of such a decision—or she could change how she (and then they) interacted.

As Patricia thought about the story she was telling herself about the divorce option, she realized that she ran the risk of seeing it as an easy escape performed by lots of people around her. She was beginning to emphasize its positive elements in her mind (relief from the constant struggle and feelings of loneliness) and avoided acknowledging the likely negatives. The truth was a lot more mixed. She later learned, for example, that people of her education level and marrying age divorced only 23 percent of the time—not the 50 percent she had always heard.[6] Apparently divorce was somewhat the exception, not the norm. What if she could find a third way—not the status quo and not a complete split, but a better, healthier relationship? Perhaps she should continue to give her new vital behaviors a try.

SOURCE 2: DO WHAT YOU CAN'T

Great relationships take skill. The illusion that the key to a successful marriage lies in the selection of the right mate prompts too many of us to leap from one relationship to the next while hoping that one day we'll find the right fit. But there's no science behind this particular strategy. In fact, the science of healthy relationships points in precisely the opposite direction.

Selection Fails. Second marriages are 34 percent less likely to succeed than first ones. The odds of making it in the third drop by another 10 percent.[7] If there was anything to the selection theory, you'd think we'd get more skilled at selection with practice. But it doesn't work out that way.

Skills Work. Marriage scholar Howard Markman has shown that a modest investment in improving conflict-management skills to help couples during their crucial moments reduces the odds of breakup by 50 percent![8]

And the key to improving one's relationship skills lies in *deliberate practice.* In the chapter "Source 2: Do What You Can't" we saw how

Patricia arranged for Jonathan to be her coach while she practiced applying crucial conversation skills to the problems she needed to solve at work. This "work practice" also gave both her and Jonathan a chance to talk about how they talked.

It came as a surprise to both Jonathan and Patricia that if they hoped to improve their relationship, they'd have to develop new skills. But then they realized that, like the rest of us, they had learned most of their relationship skills at home. This wasn't good news. In Patricia's case, her outspoken parents continually demonstrated yelling followed by furniture kicking and door slamming. Jonathan, in contrast, had been raised by parents who wouldn't raise their voice if their leg caught on fire.

So they got coaching from a marriage therapist and worked on their skills together.

Patricia learned that one of her vital behaviors, shutting up, did indeed keep her from interrupting Jonathan and controlling the conversation, but simply remaining silent wasn't enough to move their conversation along. Patricia explains, "One day Jonathan thanked me for remaining quiet while he spoke, but he could tell I wasn't listening to understand; I was listening to find fault with his views. When I spoke, I never checked for understanding by rephrasing his points; instead, I aggressively jumped in with counterarguments. And you know what? Jonathan was right. I had to practice listening—with the goal of understanding, not winning."

When it came to Jonathan's skills, he had to work on speaking up rather than simply clamming up and hoping their problems would disappear. At first he would blurt out his issues in a rather aggressive way (Patricia had given him plenty of examples), but that didn't work, so he had to study and practice speaking with candor and respect—the same thing Patricia was trying to improve.

SOURCES 3 AND 4: TURN ACCOMPLICES INTO FRIENDS

Redefine "Normal." Paul Amato, sociology professor at Pennsylvania State University, studies what he calls "low-conflict" divorces. According to his research, about half of all breakups take place in marriages that are going reasonably well and then one day suddenly end. When Amato looked closer, he learned that the primary predictor of these divorces was the divorce rate of the partners' parents.[9]

Now, if you're paying attention, you may be thinking, that was probably because, just like Patricia and Jonathan, they picked up bad habits from their parents. But Amato found that after accounting for the effects of poor interpersonal skills, the biggest factor in low-conflict divorces was low expectations. These couples saw it as "normal" to divorce. So they did.

For most of us, divorce has been normalized through outdated statistics. We've heard for years that half of marriages end in divorce. Think for a moment how knowing that number might affect your marriage, how it might color your decision about either giving it 100 percent or taking an off-ramp. Compare that to how you might weigh your options if you knew that just under one in five marriages end in their first twenty years. Would that make a difference? For many it would. In fact the 50 percent statistic was based on tracking of marriages beginning in the 1950s, when most women married before the age of twenty-one.

Today, according to marriage author Tara Parker-Pope, there's much more hope for marriage lasting than has been portrayed by the popular media.[10] The "normal" age at first marriage is now twenty-six, and analysis that began in the 1970s shows a twenty-year divorce rate of only 19 percent for college graduates who married after age twenty-five.[11]

Now, once again, we're not passing judgment on anyone's decision to remain married or divorce. This is a deeply personal choice, and there are clearly times when the wisest course of action is to end a troubled or unhealthy relationship. In these circumstances we often need social support from others to recognize that a relationship should end. In fact, recent research that we conducted at the Change Anything Labs revealed that it sometimes takes *more* social influence to help couples make the decision to end a bad relationship than it does to help them decide to keep on trying.[12]

What we want to point out is that although terminating or recommitting to a relationship is a personal choice, it's rarely made without a great deal of social influence. If you want to make the choice that is best for you, you must be aware of the powerful impact that not only your perception of what's "normal" but also the active opinions of those around you can have on your decision.

A couple of years back the Change Anything Labs conducted a Marriage on the Rocks study of 350 couples who had gone through a period where they had considered splitting up. We were startled to find that the severity of the problems they faced was not the only predictor of termination. The words of friends had a huge impact as well. According to the couples we studied, about a third of the weight in their divorce decision was determined by the words of encouragement of close friends, independent of how bad things were in the relationship.

At least one implication of this finding should be clear: If you've decided that you want to make your relationship work, you had better get your loved ones and acquaintances pulling for you. Take a careful look at those around you. Who is a friend to the relationship? Who might be an accomplice to a breakup? If necessary, have a *transformation conversation* with those who are pushing you to go separate ways. Share your struggles and goals and ask for their support—or at least neutralize the negative effects.

This isn't a new idea. One of the most consistent findings in our Marriage on the Rocks study was that coaches had a huge impact on helping to get relationships back on track.[13] Almost every one of the couples who were contemplating divorce but found a way to make their relationship work relied on the encouragement and enabling influence of someone they both trusted. It was essential that these coaches—whether they were counselors, religious leaders, or trusted friends—be seen as neutral parties in the blame game. If they began to take sides, they became more accomplice than friend.

Let's see how this plays itself out with Patricia, who, in one of her darkest times, left home. She had no intention of abandoning her children, and she was not yet ready to file for divorce. However, she was close. Patricia had looked at her default future, and all she saw was the never-ending burden of loneliness and providing for and leading the family. So one October morning, Patricia left chilly Minneapolis and flew to San Luis Obispo to spend a week with her brother. That trip made all the difference.

Now, consider how stressed-out people typically plan such a trip.

They're at an emotional low and want real help—but they tend to find buddies who console them by sympathizing with their plight. They find people who will defend rather than teach them. Rather than helping them examine their own role in the mess, the people they turn to routinely confirm their suspicions that they are innocent victims and, given half a chance, can't wait to make their life partners out as villains.

True friends, in contrast, provide clarity and wisdom as much as consolation, and that's what happened with Patricia. She spent a week with her brother, Tom, who had such an interest in marriage and family counseling that he eventually became an expert in the field. The week in San Luis Obispo was one of the most illuminating of Patricia's life. Her brother helped her understand that her own behavior might be affecting her relationship with her husband— and causing the very response from him that drove her nuts. At the same time, Tom and his wife gave Patricia space, loved her, and held her hand.

Far too often we think we ourselves are making the right decision when what we're really doing is making the decision our coaches want for us. That's normal. We seek advice, and then we use it to make choices. However, what differentiates savvy folks from the rest of us is the caution they employ when choosing counselors and coaches. They look for skilled (more often than not, trained) individuals who will provide them with a better view of themselves and a more informed set of options. Real friends provide honest feedback and actionable strategies. Accomplices—well intended though they may be—tend to join in the "ain't-he-or-she-awful" game and only make matters worse.

When you're booking your equivalent of a flight to San Luis Obispo, be sure you're headed toward wise friends and not accomplices.

SOURCE 5: INVERT THE ECONOMY

Once Patricia and Jonathan co-developed their plan for change, they decided to use incentives to help keep them on track. Both were acutely aware that the cost of a divorce would be great. For instance, women experience a 73 percent decrease in their standard of living within the first year after a divorce or permanent separation. Men usually emerge the poorer as well—particularly in those marriages where dual incomes enriched the entire family.[14]

But that wasn't the reason they chose to work through their problems. Financial hardship was in the back of their minds, but it wasn't the driving force. So, instead of looking at the cost of dissolving their marriage, Patricia and Jonathan used small rewards to help them mark and celebrate progress with their vital behaviors. They would celebrate a good week (one where they were consistent in enacting their vital behaviors) with a special night out or a favorite bottle of wine. Creating some short-term rewards for good behavior is a great way to punctuate early wins and to draw more attention to what is improving.

SOURCE 6: CONTROL YOUR SPACE

In some ways, Patricia and Jonathan's troubles can be traced to their lovely home. The large mortgage that came with it drove Patricia to work long

hours—leaving little time for the marriage. She was out the door by six thirty a.m. and walked straight to her bed at nine thirty p.m. many nights. As her relationship with Jonathan grew icier, it took a while before the two realized that their schedule— deeply affected by their home choice—had created distance that made communication less frequent and more stressful.

As Patricia created her change plan, one of her first conversations with Jonathan was about the need to change their environment. Successful Changers do the same. They use physical factors to help them enable (sometimes even make inevitable) their vital behaviors. For example:

Manage Distance. Some couples choose to *increase* their distance during the early stages of emotional turmoil in order to allow their emotions to die down. Taking a mutually agreed-upon time-out can help make good behavior easier and bad behavior harder.

As was the case with Patricia and Jonathan, many couples also make key changes in their schedule, home size and location, and life habits to find more time together. It turns out that rarely does distance make the heart grow fonder. Only proximity (coupled with good behavior) can do that.

Build Fences. One of the best things you can do for any relationship is to fence off harsh verbal conflict. Create conversation rules that exclude the opportunity for withdrawal, insults, and interruptions. For example, one of our Changer couples flipped a coin to decide who would go first.

The "winner" could voice concerns for five minutes (moderated by an actual timer). When the five minutes were over, the other partner then summarized the key concerns until the first speaker felt understood. Next, the second partner took a five-minute turn followed by the same summary process.

The two agreed that their goal would not be to solve things per se, but rather to understand one another. And yet this simple process of seeking understanding led to many more solutions as well. Creating safe and fenced-off pathways for the conversation through agreed-upon structured rules closed off dangerous off-ramps and kept their behavior productive and healthy.

Use Cues. Sometimes couples' problems recur in the same location. The two might hold a heated debate in the kitchen, or the living room might be their choice of venue. Over time these locations can send out cues that lead to conflict. The physical space becomes so associated with trouble that it generates new problems the moment you cross the threshold.

If this is true for you, you may want to find different places to hold high-stakes conversations. You could, for example, schedule a walk around the block. Or, like Helen and Ricardo in the chapter "Source 6: Control Your Space," you could use a porch. Some couples intentionally meet in a public place, knowing that they would be too embarrassed to fight in front of witnesses.[15]

The Rest of the Story. Patricia is now four years into her change plan. Just yesterday she was reflecting on the recent past, feeling grateful that she had considered the possibility that changing *her* could change *them*. Because it has.

To be realistic, not everything has changed. For example, as she was taking stock of their progress, she turned to Jonathan and said, "Am I easier to live with than I used to be?"

Jonathan is still a guy whose native tongue is silence. He hasn't become Chatty Cathy. He's deliberate and considered with his expressions. However, after a brief pause he said, "Yes."

Patricia smiled as though he had just delivered a soliloquy. Then, uncoaxed, Jonathan added, "You're a lot more patient with me. Thank you."

One of their newer rituals is a movie night. The two don't own a television, so they watch a movie on their computer. But as the days get longer and the evenings more beautiful, they'll sometimes never get to the movie because they get lost in conversation. Patricia says, "I feel as though I have a freedom with Jonathan that I hadn't recognized until now. I can tell him things that bother me and things that puzzle me— even about *him*!"

Some small changes in Patricia's behavior have profoundly changed their relationship and have facilitated Jonathan's changes as well.

HOW ABOUT YOU?

To illustrate how the principles and skills of *Change Anything* can apply to a relationship, we've dived into the personal affairs of two people who were kind enough to share their story with us. But how about you? What if you looked at the role you're playing in your current relationship—both at work and at home? Are there actions you could stop or start that might help you create more of the relationship you want?

Sure, others need to change. Not all the responsibility is yours. Then again, you are the person over whom you have most control. Can you think of your crucial moments—when things go south? Is there something you're doing to add to the problem? What vital behavior should you set to make sure that you don't make the same mistake again? What sources of influence might you put in place to ensure that you stay the course? Once you start developing a personal plan, why not learn from others who are doing the same? Log on to ChangeAnything.com and learn what others have done to strengthen their bonds.

Conclusion
How to Change the World

Before you set this book down, we want to make sure that you quickly and effectively get started with your own personal change effort—and maybe a bigger effort as well. To do so, we offer the following pieces of advice.

1. ACT SMALL, ACT NOW

We've given you a careful way of thinking about the science of personal change. We've told you about crucial moments, vital behaviors, six powerful sources of influence, and the need to learn and adjust. Following this advice can seem so overwhelming that you might be tempted to put off getting started for another day—or decade.

Don't. Following the advice may not be nearly as difficult as it appears. For example, while change will happen when you align all six sources in support of your new habits, you might already have more of the sources working in your favor than you think. Many people succeed by simply adding one more source of influence.

For example, simply start using smaller plates and utensils, and you may start shedding pounds like you've always hoped.

Turn one accomplice into a friend, and you may get over the hump in your goal of quitting smoking.

Transform your career goal into a game by breaking it into small wins and creating a way to keep score, and you may get traction in no time.

There is absolutely nothing wrong with starting your attempt to move forward by simply adding an idea or two from this book to whatever you've been doing before. View the Change Anything model as a way of improving your plan incrementally over time.

Just get started. Learn from both your successes and your failures, and then adjust. Eventually you'll discover the right combination of tactics to help you change for good.

2. RECORD IT

Second, don't forget the important research we shared in the chapter "Be the Scientist and the Subject." One of your most potent change tools is a recording device—pens, pencils, laptops. Simply recording a plan increases your chance of success by almost a third!

If you haven't gone there yet, take advantage of your free access to ChangeAnything.com by typing in the code found inside your book cover. It's never been easier to create, record, and begin a customized change plan based on the best advice science has to offer. Even if you're not ready to begin right now, browsing the plans and experiences of others may help you decide what and when you want to change.

3. IMAGINE

The material contained in this book can also be used to influence others—friends, co-workers, communities, companies, anything that is populated with human beings. We chose to write about personal change in this book, but in its predecessor (*Influencer: The Power to Change Anything*) we applied the same model to changing others. We showed how the science you now understand has been used to bring about changes most of the world thought were impossible.

For example, we showed how one man with very little formal authority was able to change the behavior of sixty million of his countrymen in order to reduce AIDS infections by close to 90 percent. And he did it in just a couple of years. We introduced the world to a woman who has helped more than fifteen thousand hardened criminals become productive, law-abiding citizens. We revealed the influence principles behind the remarkable work of an ordinary citizen who influenced U.S. health care workers to save one hundred thousand lives from medical mistakes.

We share this because we want you to know that, like the people just described, you can apply the change tools you've just studied to problems of all kinds, to people of all kinds. The six sources of influence affect all human behavior—including that of the individuals around you. Imagine if you applied the six sources to solving crime, increasing the quality of education, eradicating diseases... there are no limits to what can be done.

Think about it. What would this world be like if there were a million more people who knew how to apply good science to human change? Lots of important problems would be solved. That's because *when you aim at vital behaviors and get all six sources of influence working in your favor, you change. When you motivate and enable others to enact their vital behaviors, they change.*

4. CHANGE THE WORLD

We began this book by suggesting that our intent was not simply to write a good book, but to help you create change. We hope first and foremost that reading this book has increased your ability to succeed at changing something meaningful to you. More importantly, we hope you'll get started.

We give you our final assurance that while there is yet much to learn about human change, you now have a basic grasp of how to make it happen far more effectively than ever before. You have a systematic way of changing anything. Our hope is that you will now go out and change *something.*

Notes

Preface

1. Change Anything Labs, *Lake Wobegon at Work* survey (February 2010).
2. Annamaria Lusardi and Olivia S. Mitchell, "Financial Literacy and Planning: Implications for Retirement Wellbeing," Netherlands Central Bank, Research Department, January 2006. Only 19 percent of people age fifty or older who were surveyed had engaged in any kind of effective retirement planning.
3. Change Anything Labs, *Marriage on the Rocks* survey (November 2009). See also Kurt Hahlweg, Howard J. Markman, Franz Thurmaier, Jochen Engl, and Volker Eckert, "Prevention of Marital Distress: Results of a German Prospective Longitudinal Study," *Journal of Family Psychology* 12, no. 4 (December 1998): 543–556.
4. Stanton Peele, *7 Tools to Beat Addiction* (New York: Three Rivers Press, 2004).
5. Joseph Grenny, David Maxfield, and Andrew Shimberg, "How to Have Influence," *MIT Sloan Management Review* (October 1, 2008): 47–52.
6. Change Anything Labs, *Personal Problems at Work* survey of 679 managers and executives (March 2010). See also Arlene A. Johnson, "The

Business Case for Work-Family Programs," *Journal of Accountancy* 180, no. 2 (August 1995): 53–59.

Escape the Willpower Trap

1. Albert Bandura and Walter Mischel, "Modification of Self-Imposed Delay of Reward through Exposure to Live and Symbolic Models," *Journal of Personality and Social Psychology* 2, no. 1 (1965): 698–705.

2. Bill Friedman, *Designing Casinos to Dominate the Competition: The Friedman International Standards of Casino Design* (Reno, NV: Institute for the Study of Gambling and Commercial Gaming College of Business Administration, 2000).

3. Jeffrey Kluger, "Neural Advertising: The Sounds We Can't Resist," *Time*, March 1, 2010.

4. Former employee of the North Rim Grand Canyon Lodge, conversation with Kerry Patterson (August 1967).

5. Change Anything Labs, *Friends and Accomplices* study (November 2009). See also J.F. Finch, M.A. Okun, G.J. Pool, and L.S. Ruehlman, "A Comparison of the Influence of Conflictual and Supportive Social Interactions on Psychological Distress," *Journal of Personality*, 67 (August 1999): 581– 621; Manuel Barrera Jr., Laurie Chassin, and Fred Rogosch, "Effects of Social Support and Conflict on Adolescent Children of Alcoholic and Nonalcoholic Fathers," *Journal of Personality*, 64 (April 1993): 602–612.

Be the Scientist and the Subject

1. John M. Gottman and Nan Silver, *The Seven Principles for Making Marriage Work* (London: Orion, 2000).

2. Change Anything Labs, *Lake Wobegon at Work* survey (February 2010).

3. Change Anything Labs, *Influencing Behavior Change* survey (October 2007).

4. Jenny McCune, "Does Debt Consolidation Work?" CNBC.com, December 10, 2009, http://www.cnbc.com/id/34365857/Does_Debt_Consoli dation_ Work.

5. Julie Rawe, "Science of Appetite: Fat Chance," *Time*, http://www.time.com/ time/specials/2007/article/0,28804,1626795_1627112_1626456,00.html.

6. Christopher D. Gardner, Alexandre Kiazand, Sofiya Alhassan, Soowon Kim, Randall S. Stafford, Raymond R. Balise, Helena C. Kraemer, and Abby C. King, "Comparison of the Atkins, Zone, Ornish, and LEARN Diets for Change in Weight and Related Risk Factors among Overweight Premenopausal Women: The A to Z Weight Loss Study: A Randomized Trial," *Journal of the American Medical Association* 297, no. 9 (2007): 969–977.

7. Peter Gollwitzer and Paschal Sheeran, "Implementation Intentions and Goal Achievement: A Meta-Analysis of Effects and Processes," *Advances in Experimental Social Psychology* 38 (2006): 69–119.

8. Ibid.

9. P. Sheeran, T. Webb, and P.M. Gollwitzer, "The Interplay between Goal Intentions and Implementation Intentions," *Personality and Social Psychology Bulletin* 31 (2005): 87–98.

10. R. Cialdini and N. Goldstein, "Social Influence: Compliance and Conformity," *Annual Review of Psychology* 55 (2004): 591–621.

Source 1: Love What You Hate

1. Daniel Read and Barbara van Leeuwen, "Predicting Hunger: The Effects of Appetite and Delay on Choice," *Organizational Behavior and Human Decision Processes* 76, no. 2 (1998): 189–205.

2. To learn more about the extraordinary work Valter and his colleagues complete, watch Lucy Walker's award-winning documentary *Waste Land* (London: Almega Projects, 2010).

3. Hans Gruber, Petra Jansen, Jörg Marienhagen, and Eckart Altenmüller, "Adaptations during the Acquisition of Expertise," *Talent Development and Excellence* 1, no. 2 (2009): 3–15.

4. Ruth Helman, Craig Copeland, and Jack VanDerhei, "The 2010 Retirement Confidence Survey: Confidence Stabilizing, but Preparations Continue to Erode," EBRI Issue Brief, no. 340 (March 2010).

5. Ongoing research in Ghana by Dean Karlan, professor of economics at Yale University, showed that those using labeled accounts saved an average of 50 percent more than those with traditional unlabeled accounts.

6. V. Liberman, S.M. Samuels, and L. Ross, "The Name of the Game: Predictive Power of Reputations versus Situational Labels in Determining Prisoner's Dilemma Game Moves," *Personality and Social Psychology Bulletin* 30, no. 9 (2004): 1175–1185.

7. "Importance of Insulin Delivery Devices for Diabetes Management," *ScienceDaily* (June 15, 2010).

8. You can find some great examples of Personal Motivation Statements at ChangeAnything.com/exclusive.

9. S.M. Colby, P.M. Monti, N.P. Barnett, D.J. Rohsenow, A. Spirito, R. Woolard, M. Myers, and W. Lewander, "Motivational Interviewing for Alcohol-Related Emergencies: Outcome for 13–17 Year Olds" (paper presented at the symposium Brief Motivational Interventions in the Emergency Department for Adolescents and Adults, chaired by R. Longabaugh and P.M. Monti, at the annual meeting of the Research Society on Alcoholism, Santa Barbara, CA, June 1999).

Source 2: Do What You Can't

1. Sara Gable and Susan Lutz, "Household, Parent, and Child Contributions to Childhood Obesity," *Family Relations* 49 (2004): 293–300.

2. Richard L. Wiener, Corinne Baron-Donovan, Karen Gross, and Susan Block-Lieb, "Debtor Education, Financial Literacy, and Pending Bankruptcy Legislation," *Behavioral Sciences and the Law* 23 (2005): 347–366.

3. M.V. William, D.W. Baker, E.G. Honig, T.M. Lee, and A. Nowlan, "Inadequate Literacy Is a Barrier to Asthma Knowledge and Self-Care," *Chest* 114 (1998): 1008–1015.

4. Change Anything Labs, *Lake Wobegon at Work* survey (February 2010).

5. Albert Bandura, Robert Jeffery, and Carolyn Wright, "Efficacy of Participant Modeling as a Function of Response Induction Aids," *Journal of Abnormal Psychology* 83, no. 1 (1974): 56–64.

6. K.A. Ericsson, R.Th. Krampe, and C. Tesch-Römer, "The Role of Deliberate Practice in the Acquisition of Expert Performance," *Psychological Review* 100 (1993): 363–406.

7. K. Anders Ericsson, Neil Charness, Paul Feltovich, and Robert Hoffman, *The Cambridge Handbook of Expertise and Expert Performance* (Cambridge University Press, 2006).

8. Jeffrey Schwartz and Sharon Begley, *The Mind and the Brain: Neuroplasticity and the Power of Mental Force* (London: HarperCollins, 2004).

9. Anne Fletcher, *Sober for Good* (New York: Houghton Mifflin Harcourt, 2001); Frederick Rotgers, Marc Kern, and Rudy Hoetzel, *Responsible Drinking: A Moderation Management Approach for Problem Drinkers* (Oakland, CA: New Harbinger, 2002).

Sources 3 and 4: Turn Accomplices into Friends

1. S.E. Asch, "Effects of Group Pressure upon the Modification and Distortion of Judgment," in *Groups, Leadership, and Men*, ed. H. Guetzkow (Pittsburgh, PA: Carnegie Press, 1951).

2. S. Milgram, *Obedience to Authority: An Experimental View* (London: Pinter & Martin Ltd, 2010).

3. Martin T. Orne and Frederick J. Evans, "Social Control in the Psychological Experiment: Antisocial Behavior and Hypnosis," *Journal of Personality and Social Psychology* 1, no. 3 (1965): 189–200.

4. Nicholas A. Christakis, MD, PhD, MPH, and James H. Fowler, PhD, "The Spread of Obesity in a Large Social Network over 32 Years," *New England Journal of Medicine* 357 (July 26, 2007): 370–379.

5. David Maxfield, Joseph Grenny, Ron McMillan, Kerry Patterson, and Al Switzler, *Silence Kills: The Seven Crucial Conversations for Healthcare* (Provo, UT: VitalSmarts, 2005), 2.

6. Patti Neighmond, "Impact of Childhood Obesity Goes Beyond Health," NPR, July 8, 2010, http://www.npr.org/templates/story/story .php?storyId=128804121.

7. Julia Hanf, "Minimizing the Negative Health Effects of Diabetes," What-Is-Diabetes.org, July 22, 2008, http://what-is-diabetes.org/diabetes/ minimizing-the-negative-health-effects-of-diabetes/.

8. Kaiser Permanente, the MIT Media Lab, and a few other organizations recently supported the formation of the Care Product Institute (CPI), a nonprofit group pioneering ways to combine "technology with social support," according to CPI's Brent Lowenshohn, an authority on health care technology. In the CPI model, a diabetic's glucose reading might be transmitted to a designated relative who is trained to know what that number means and what to do about it. The family member can then nudge the patient to take appropriate actions. Amy Salzhauer, "Forethought Frontiers: Is There a Patient in the House?" *Harvard Business Review* (November 2005): 32.

9. Research suggests that texting while driving increases the risk of accident by twenty-three times. Jennifer Guevin, "Study: Texting While Driving Increases Crash Risk 23-fold," *CNET News*, July 27, 2009.

10. Change Anything Labs, *Friends and Accomplices* study (November 2009).

Source 5: Invert the Economy

1. Eric A. Finkelstein, Justin G. Trogdon, Joel W. Cohen, and William Dietz, "Annual Medical Spending Attributable to Obesity: Payer- and Service-Specific Estimates," *Health Affairs* 28, no. 5 (2009): 822–831.
2. J.L. Zagorsky, "Marriage and Divorce's Impact on Wealth," *Journal of Sociology* 41, no. 4 (2005): 406–424.
3. Change Anything Labs, *Lake Wobegon at Work* survey (February 2010).
4. Stanton Peele, *7 Tools to Beat Addiction* (New York: Three Rivers Press, 2004), 96.
5. The study *Tobacco Taxes: A WIN-WIN-WIN for Cash-Strapped States* (February 10, 2010) was published by the Campaign for Tobacco-Free Kids, American Heart Association, American Cancer Society Cancer Action Network, American Lung Association, and the Robert Wood Johnson Foundation.
6. Daniel Kahneman, Jack L. Knetsch, and Richard H. Thaler, "Anomalies: The Endowment Effect, Loss Aversion, and Status Quo Bias," *Journal of Economic Perspectives* 5, no. 1 (Winter 1991): 193–206.
7. Study done by Change Anything Labs in July 2010 with eighty-five customers awaiting release of the iPhone 4 at the Salt Lake City, Utah, Apple store. See also Daniel Kahneman, Jack L. Knetsch, and Richard H. Thaler, "Experimental Tests of the Endowment Effect and the Coase Theorem," *Journal of Political Economy* 98, no. 6 (December 1998): 1325–1348.
8. Xavier Giné, Dean S. Karlan, and Jonathan Zinman, "Put Your Money Where Your Butt Is: A Commitment Contract for Smoking Cessation" (July 1, 2009). World Bank Policy Research Working Paper Series, 4985.

9. Gina Pace, "Life after 'Loser': 'Every Day Is a Struggle,' " MSNBC, January 5, 2009, http://today.msnbc.msn.com/id/28449267.

10. Victoria Lee Miller, "Will Kirstie Alley's Weight Gain Hurt Jenny Craig?" *Associated Content*, May 12, 2009, http://www.associatedcontent.com/article/1702649/will_kirstie_alleys_weight_gain_hurt.html.

11. Mark R. Lepper, David Greene, and Richard E. Nisbett, "Undermining Children's Intrinsic Interest with Extrinsic Reward: A Test of the 'Overjustification Hypothesis.' " *Journal of Personality and Social Psychology* 28 (1973): 129–137.

12. Albert Bandura and Karen Simon, "The Role of Proximal Intentions in Self-Regulation of Refractory Behavior," *Cognitive Therapy and Research* 1, no. 3 (1977): 177–193.

13. Albert Bandura and Dale Schunk, "Cultivating Competence, Self-Efficacy, and Intrinsic Interest through Proximal Self-Motivation," *Journal of Personality and Social Psychology* 41, no. 3 (1981): 586–598.

Source 6: Control Your Space

1. Brian Wansink, *Mindless Eating: Why We Eat More Than We Think* (London: Hay House, 2011).

2. S.J. Hoch and G.F. Loewenstein, "Time-Inconsistent Preferences and Consumer Self-Control," *Journal of Consumer Research* 17 (1991): 1–16.

3. Anna Breman, "Give More Tomorrow: Two Field Experiments on Altruism and Intertemporal Choice" (submitted paper, Stockholm University, November 2, 2006).

4. Bob Edwards, "Hearty Diets, Hard Labor Keep Amish Fit," *Morning Edition*, NPR, January 14, 2004.

5. Nielsen, *Three Screen Report: Television, Internet, and Mobile Usage in the U.S.* 5 (second quarter 2009); Norman Herr, "Television and Health,"

Internet Resources to Accompany the Sourcebook for Teaching Science, California State University, 2007, http://www.csun.edu/science/health/ docs/tv&health.html?.
6. Some popular finance applications include LearnVest.com and Mint.com.
7. "Dining Room Table Losing Central Status in Families," *USA Today*, December 18, 2005.

Career: How to Get Unstuck at Work

1. Change Anything Labs, *Lake Wobegon at Work* survey (February 2010).
2. Daniel Yankelovich and John Immerwahr, *Putting the Work Ethic to Work: A Public Agenda's Report on Restoring America's Competitive Vitality* (New York: Public Agenda Foundation, 1983).
3. This finding is from a 2002 study of fifteen hundred software engineers at a client organization.
4. Jeffrey Pfeffer, *Managing with Power: Politics and Influence in Organizations* (Boston: Harvard Business School Press, 1994), 154.

Weight Loss: How to Lose Weight and Get Fit—and Stay That Way

1. Paul M. Johnson and Paul J. Kenny, "Dopamine D2 Receptors in Addiction-like Reward Dysfunction and Compulsive Eating in Obese Rats," *Nature Neuroscience* (2010), doi:10.1038/nn.2519.
2. Ibid.
3. Sarah Klein, "Fatty Foods May Cause Cocaine-like Addiction," *CNN*, March 30, 2010, http://articles.cnn.com/2010-03-28/health/fatty.foods .brain_1_rats-junk-food-fatty-foods?_s=PM:HEALTH.
4. Barry M. Popkin, "The World Is Fat," *Scientific American*, September 2007.

5. National Eating Disorders Association, *kNOw Dieting: Risks and Reasons to Stop* (Seattle, WA: National Eating Disorders Association, 2005), http://www.nationaleatingdisorders.org.

6. Christopher D. Gardner, Alexandre Kiazand, Sofiya Alhassan, Soowon Kim, Randall S. Stafford, Raymond R. Balise, Helena C. Kraemer, and Abby C. King, "Comparison of the Atkins, Zone, Ornish, and LEARN Diets for Change in Weight and Related Risk Factors among Overweight Premenopausal Women: The A to Z Weight Loss Study: A Randomized Trial," *Journal of the American Medical Association* 297, no. 9 (2007): 969–977.

7. Daniel Gilbert, *Stumbling on Happiness* (London: Harper Perennial, 2007).

8. Jeffrey Schwartz and Sharon Begley, *The Mind and the Brain: Neuroplasticity and the Power of Mental Force* (London: HarperCollins, 2004).

9. Change Anything Labs, *Friends and Accomplices* study (November 2009).

10. Abby C. King, Robert Friedman, Bess Marcus, Cynthia Castro, Melissa Napolitano, David Ahn, and Lawrence Baker, "Ongoing Physical Activity Advice by Humans versus Computers: The Community Health Advice by Telephone (CHAT) Trial," *Health Psychology* 26, no. 6 (2007): 718–727.

Financial Fitness: How to Get—and Live—Out of Debt

1. The number of adults age sixty-five or over living with their children has increased 62 percent over the past decade. "More Parents Move In with Kids," *USA Today*, September 23, 2008.

2. Kim Khan, "How Does Your Debt Compare?" *MSN Money*, http://moneycentral.msn.com/content/savinganddebt/p70581.asp.

3. Brian O'Connell, "Debt Counseling Helps Bankrupt Americans," *Main-Street Newsletter,* June 17, 2010.

4. Barbara O'Neill, "Danger Signals of Excessive Debt," Cornell Cooperative Extension, September 20, 2009, http://www.extension.org/pages/Danger_Signals_of_Excessive_Debt.

5. Dave Ramsey, *The Total Money Makeover* (Nashville, TN: Thomas Nelson, 2009).

6. Paco Underhill, *Why We Buy: The Science of Shopping* (New York: Simon and Schuster, 1999).

7. William R. Miller and Stephen Rollnick, *Motivational Interviewing* (New York: Guilford Press, 2002), 5–7, 220, 226. Go to ChangeAnything.com/exclusive to download a handy guide on holding a motivational interview.

8. Haiyang Chen and Ronald P. Volpe, "An Analysis of Personal Financial Literacy Among College Students," *Financial Services Review* 7, no. 2 (1998): 107–128.

9. Piyush Sharma, Bharadhwaj Sivakumaran, and Roger Marshall, "Impulse Buying and Variety Seeking: A Trait-Correlates Perspective," *Journal of Business Research* 63, no. 3 (March 2010): 276–283.

10. Daniel Gilbert, *Stumbling on Happiness* (London: Harper Perennial, 2007).

11. Control direct mail and catalogs by registering online at the Direct Marketing Association's website. There is no fee for online registration. Visit https://www.dmachoice.org/dma/member/regist.action. Stop receiving credit card applications by registering at OptOutPreScreen.com.

Addiction: How to Take Back Your Life

1. L.N. Robins, "Vietnam Veterans' Rapid Recovery from Heroin Addiction: Fluke or Normal Expectation?" *Addiction* 88 (1993): 1041–1054.

2. J. Olds and P. Milner, "Positive Reinforcement Produced by Electrical Stimulation of Septal Area and Other Regions of Rat Brain," *Journal of*

Comparative and Physiological Psychology 47, no. 6 (December 1954): 419–427.

3. K.C. Berridge, T.E. Robinson, and J.W. Aldridge, "Dissecting Components of Reward: 'Liking,' 'Wanting,' and Learning," *Current Opinion in Pharmacology* 9 (2009): 1–9.

4. T.E. Robinson and K.C. Berridge, "The Neural Basis of Drug Craving: An Incentive-Sensitization Theory of Addiction," *Brain Research Reviews* 18 (1993): 247–291.

5. "After Lung Cancer Surgery, Nearly Half of Patients Resume Smoking," *LiveScience*, December 11, 2006, http://www.livescience.com/health/061211_smokers_resume.html.

6. G. Alan Marlatt, "A Cognitive-Behavioral Model of the Relapse Process," in *Behavioral Analysis and Treatment of Substance Abuse*, National Institute on Drug Abuse research monograph 25, ed. N.A. Krasnegor (Washington, DC: U.S. Government Printing Office, 1979), 191–200.

7. J.R. Hughes, "Alcohol Withdrawal Seizures," *Epilepsy Behavior* 15, no. 2 (February 2009): 92–97.

8. Stanton Peele, *7 Tools to Beat Addiction* (New York: Three Rivers Press, 2004).

9. Christopher J. Mruk, *Self-Esteem Research, Theory, and Practice: Toward a Positive Psychology of Self-Esteem* (New York: Springer, 2006).

10. John J. Ratey, *Spark: The Revolutionary New Science of Exercise and the Brain* (London: Quercus Publishing, 2010).

11. Ibid.

12. Steven Kipnis and Joy Davidoff, *Nicotine Dependence and Smoking Cessation* (Albany: New York State Office of Alcoholism and Substance Abuse Services, OASAS Addiction Medicine Unit, 2003).

13. A.H. Taylor, M.H. Ussher, and G. Faulkner, "The Acute Effects of Exercise on Cigarette Cravings, Withdrawal Symptoms, Affect and Smoking Behaviour: A Systematic Review," *Addiction* 102 (2007): 534–543.

14. Kimberly S. Young and Robert C. Rogers, "The Relationships between Depression and Internet Addiction," *Cyber Psychology and Behavior* 1, no. 1 (1998): 25–28.

15. Robert F. Anda, David F. Williamson, Luis G. Escobedo, Eric E. Mast, Gary A. Giovino, and Patrick L. Remington, "Depression and the Dynamics of Smoking," *Journal of the American Medical Association* 264 (1990): 1541–1545.

Relationships: How to Change Us by Changing Me

1. D.A. Redelmeier, J. Katz, and D. Kahneman, "Memories of Colonoscopy: A Randomized Trial," *Pain* 104 (July 2003): 187–194.

2. John Gottman and Nan Silver, *The Seven Principles for Making Marriage Work* (London: Orion, 2000).

3. Clifford Notarius and Howard Markman, *We Can Work It Out: How to Solve Conflicts, Save Your Marriage* (New York: Berkley, 1993), 31.

4. Gottman and Silver, *Seven Principles*, 160.

5. Tara Parker-Pope, *For Better: The Science of a Good Marriage* (London: Vermilion, 2010), 128.

6. Ibid., chap. 1.

7. Ibid.

8. Notarius and Markman, *We Can Work It Out*, 11.

9. Paul Amato and Bryndl Hohmann-Marriott, "A Comparison of High-and Low-Distress Marriages That End in Divorce," *Journal of Marriage and Family* 69 (August 2007): 621–638.

10. Parker-Pope, *For Better*.

11. Betsey Stevenson and Julian Wolfers, "Marriage and Divorce: Changes and Their Driving Forces," *Journal of Economic Perspectives* 21, no. 2 (Spring 2007): 27–52.

12. Change Anything Labs, *Marriage on the Rocks* survey (November 2009).

13. Ibid.

14. Patricia A. McManus and Thomas A. DiPrete, "Losers and Winners: The Financial Consequences of Separation and Divorce for Men," *American Sociological Review* 66, no. 2 (April 2001): 246–268.

15. Michele Weiner-Davis, *Divorce Busting: A Step-by-Step Approach to Making Your Marriage Loving Again* (New York: Simon and Schuster, 1992), 149.

Index

About the Authors

This award-winning team of authors has produced three *New York Times* bestsellers—*Crucial Conversations: Tools for Talking When Stakes Are High* (2002), *Crucial Confrontations: Tools for Resolving Broken Promises, Violated Expectations, and Bad Behavior* (2005), and *Influencer: The Power to Change Anything* (2008).

Kerry Patterson has authored award-winning training programs and led multiple long-term change efforts. In 2004, he received the BYU Marriott School of Management Dyer Award for outstanding contribution in organizational behavior. He completed doctoral work at Stanford University.

Joseph Grenny is an acclaimed keynote speaker and consultant who has implemented major corporate change initiatives for the past twenty years. He is also a co-founder of Unitus, a not-for-profit organization that helps the world's poor achieve economic self-reliance.

David Maxfield is a leading researcher, consultant, and speaker. He has led research studies on the role of human behavior in medical errors, safety hazards, and project execution. He completed doctoral work in psychology at Stanford University.

Ron McMillan is a sought-after speaker and consultant. He co-founded the Covey Leadership Center, where he served as vice president of research and development. He has worked with leaders ranging from first-level managers to executives from the *Fortune* 500.

Al Switzler is a renowned consultant and speaker who has directed training and management initiatives with leaders from dozens of *Fortune* 500 companies worldwide. He is also on the faculty of the Executive Development Center at the University of Michigan.

Want to get better?
Award-winning Training
from **Vital**Smarts

Change Anything Training™

Take charge of the change you'd like to see in your personal or professional life. Create a complete change plan and remove the barriers to your success.

Influencer Training™

Uproot entrenched habits and drive rapid and sustainable behavior change within teams and even entire organizations.

Crucial Conversations® Training

Drive results by learning to speak with complete candor and complete respect—no matter the issues or the individuals involved.

Crucial Confrontations® Training

Ensure flawless execution with this step-by-step process for improving accountability and addressing performance.

To receive more information on training
from VitalSmarts,
go online to **www.VitalSmarts.com/global**

About **Vital**Smarts

An innovator in corporate training and organizational performance, VitalSmarts helps teams and organizations achieve the results they care about most. With award-winning training products based on more than thirty years of ongoing research, VitalSmarts has helped more than three hundred of the *Fortune* 500 realize significant results using a proven method for driving rapid, sustainable, and measurable change in behaviors. VitalSmarts has been ranked by *Inc.* magazine as one of the fastest-growing companies in America for the last six years and has trained more than 600,000 people worldwide.

VitalSmarts is home to multiple training offerings, including Crucial Conversations®, Crucial Confrontations®, Influencer Training™, and Change Anything Training™. Each course improves key organizational outcomes by focusing on high-leverage skills and strategies. Along with *Change Anything*, their latest title, the VitalSmarts authors have written three *New York Times* bestsellers: *Crucial Conversations*, *Crucial Confrontations*, and *Influencer*. VitalSmarts also offers on-site consulting, research, executive team development, and speaking engagements.

www.VitalSmarts.com/global

About **ChangeAnything.com**

ChangeAnything.com is a social network that helps people change chronic bad behaviors for good. Based on the ground-breaking principles in the book, *Change Anything: The New Science of Personal Success*, ChangeAnything.com guides people through their unique change challenges in their personal and professional lives. From individual to corporate change, thousands of people are dramatically increasing their probability of permanent change with ChangeAnything.com.

Change Anything LLC was founded in 2009 and is a subsidiary of VitalSmarts.

www.ChangeAnything.com

EXCLUSIVE ACCESS FOR BOOK READERS

Authors Kerry Patterson, Joseph Grenny, David Maxfield, Ron McMillan, and Al Switzler are offering book readers the following **FREE resources.** All you have to do is go online to get them. Read on.

Access the Change Anything Video Vault

From marshmallow temptations to overpriced Silly String, the authors bring the Change Anything experiments to life in these award-winning short clips. Watch as kid-scientist Hyrum Grenny teaches his peers how to increase willpower, wash their hands, and even save money!

Personal Motivation Statement Wizard

Want some help creating a compelling Personal Motivation Statement? ChangeAnything.com will walk you through the process of developing a statement that will help you reconnect with the results you do—and don't—want during your crucial moments.

Friends & Accomplices Inventory

One of the most illuminating things you can do to understand why change is so hard is to develop a Friends and Accomplices Inventory. This tool will give you a riveting and empowering picture of the social dynamic surrounding you—as well as tips for turning accomplices into friends in order to guarantee new behaviors.

Join the *Crucial Skills Newsletter* Community

Subscribe to our weekly e-newsletter and ask the authors for advice in solving pressing challenges. The authors answer a reader's question each week, providing powerful insights into the tough, real-world challenges you face.

To access these free resources, visit
www.ChangeAnything.com/exclusive

ALSO FROM THE BESTSELLING AUTHOR TEAM

"This is a breakthrough book, I found myself being deeply influenced, motivated, and even inspired."

—Stephen R. Covey, author of
The 7 Habits of Highly Effective People

"If you read only one 'management' book this decade . . . I'd insist that it be *Crucial Confrontations*."

—Tom Peters, author of *Re-Imagine!*

"Influencing human behavior is one of the most difficult challenges faced by leaders. This book provides powerful insight into how to make behavior change that will last."

—Sidney Taurel, Chairman & CEO,
Eli Lilly and Company